CW00808534

ISBN: 9781313956451

Published by:
HardPress Publishing
8345 NW 66TH ST #2561
MIAMI FL 33166-2626

Email: info@hardpress.net
Web: http://www.hardpress.net

Early English Poets.

ROBERT HERRICK.

PRINTED BY ROBERT ROBERTS
BOSTON.

Early English Poets.

THE
COMPLETE POEMS

OF

ROBERT HERRICK.

EDITED,

WITH

Memorial-Introduction and Notes,

BY THE

REV. ALEXANDER B. GROSART.

IN THREE VOLUMES.—VOL. II.

London:
CHATTO AND WINDUS, PICCADILLY.
1876.

PR
3510
A5G76
1876
15-34 ov. 2
16/9/9'

Contents.

PAGE

HESPERIDES *(continued)*

VOL. II.   a a

HESPERIDES.

How Roses came red.

 OSES at first were white,
   Till they co'd not agree,
Whether my *Sapho's* breast,
   Or they more white sho'd be.

But being vanquisht quite,
   A blush their cheeks bespred ;
Since which (beleeve the rest)
   The *Roses* first came red.

Comfort to a Lady upon the Death
of her Husband.

DRY your sweet cheek, long drown'd with sorrows
   raine ;
Since Clouds disperst, Suns guild the Aire again.
Seas chafe and fret, and beat, and over-boile ;
But turne soone after calme, as Balme, or Oile.

Winds have their time to rage ; but when they cease,
The leavie-trees nod in a still-born peace.
Your storme is over ; Lady, now appeare
Like to the peeping spring-time of the yeare.
Off then with grave clothes ; put fresh colours on ;
And flow, and flame, in your *Vermillion.*
Upon your cheek sate *Ysicles* awhile ;
Now let the Rose raigne like a Queene, and smile.

How Violets came blew.

L OVE on a day (wise Poets tell)
    Some time in wrangling spent,
Whether the Violets sho'd excell,
    Or she, in sweetest scent.
But *Venus* having lost the day,
    Poore Girles, she fell on you ;
And beat ye so, (as some dare say)
    Her blowes did make ye blew.

Upon Groynes.   *Epig.*

G *ROYNES,* for his fleshly *Burglary* of late,
    Stood in the *Holy-Forum Candidate* ;[1]
The word is *Roman ;* but in English knowne :
Penance, and standing so, are both but one.

[1] Holy Forum = church-yard : candidate, in a white sheet, doing
penance.

To the Willow-tree.

1. THOU art to all lost love the best,
   The onely true plant found,
   Wherewith young men and maids distrest,
   And left of love, are crown'd.

2. When once the Lovers Rose is dead,
   Or laid aside forlorne ;
   Then Willow-garlands, 'bout the head,
   Bedew'd with teares, are worne.

3. When with Neglect, (the Lover's bane)
   Poore Maids rewarded be,
   For their love lost ; their onely gaine
   Is but a Wreathe from thee.

4. And underneath thy cooling shade,
   (When weary of the light)
   The love-spent Youth, and love-sick Maid,
   Come to weep out the night.

Mrs. Eliz. Wheeler, *under the name of the lost Shepardesse.*[2]

AMONG the *Mirtles*, as I walkt,
Love and my sighs thus intertalkt :

[2] See Memorial-Introduction, on the mis-ascription of this to Carew.

Tell me, said I, in deep distresse,
Where I may find my Shepardesse.
Thou foole, said Love, know'st thou not this?
In every thing that's sweet, she is.
In yond' *Carnation* goe and seek,
There thou shalt find her lip and cheek :
In that ennamel'd *Pansie* by,
There thou shalt have her curious eye :
In bloome of *Peach*, and *Roses* bud,
There waves the Streamer of her blood.
'Tis true, said I, and thereupon
I went to pluck them one by one,
To make of parts an union ;
But on a sudden all were gone.
At which I stopt ; Said Love, these be
The true resemblances of thee ;
For as these flowers, thy joyes must die,
And in the turning of an eye ;
And all thy hopes of her must wither,
Like those short sweets ere knit together.

TO THE KING.

IF when these Lyricks (CESAR) You shall heare,
  And that *Apollo* shall so touch Your eare,

As for to make this, that, or any one
Number, Your owne, by free Adoption;
That Verse, of all the Verses here, shall be
The Heire to This *great Realme of Poetry.*

TO THE QUEENE.

G*ODDESSE of Youth, and Lady of the Spring,*
    (Most fit to be the Consort to a King)
Be pleas'd to rest you in *This Sacred Grove,*
Beset with *Mirtles*; whose each leafe drops Love.
Many a sweet-fac't *Wood-Nymph* here is seene,
Of which chast *Order You* are now the *Queene:*
Witnesse their *Homage,* when they come and strew
Your Walks with Flowers, and give their Crowns to
    you.
Your Leavie-Throne (with *Lilly*-work) possesse;
And be both Princesse here, and Poetresse.[3]

The Poets good wishes for the most
hopefull and handsome Prince,
the Duke of Yorke.[4]

M AY his pretty Duke-ship grow
    Like t' a Rose of *Jericho:*

[3] = poetess.
[4] James II. afterwards. He was declared Duke of York at his
birth, but was not formally so created until 27th January, 1642-3.

Sweeter far, then ever yet   [*than*
Showrs or Sun-shines co'd beget.
May the Graces, and the Howers
Strew his hopes, and Him with flowers :
And so dresse him up with Love,
As to be the Chick of *Jove.*
May the thrice-three-Sisters sing
Him the Soveraigne of their Spring :
And entitle none to be
Prince of *Hellicon*, but He.
May his soft foot, where it treads,
Gardens thence produce and Meads :
And those Meddowes full be set
With the Rose, and Violet.
May his ample Name be knowne
To the last succession :
And his actions high be told
Through the world, but writ in gold.

To Anthea, *who may command him any thing.*

1. B ID me to live, and I will live
       Thy Protestant [5] to be :
Or bid me love, and I will give
       A loving heart to thee.

[5] = protester ?

2. A heart as soft, a heart as kind,
    A heart as sound and free,
  As in the whole world thou canst find,
    That heart Ile give to thee.

3. Bid that heart stay, and it will stay,
    To honour thy Decree :
  Or bid it languish quite away,
    And't shall doe so for thee.

4. Bid me to weep, and I will weep,
    While I have eyes to see :
  And having none, yet I will keep
    A heart to weep for thee.

5. Bid me despaire, and Ile despaire,
    Under that *Cypresse* tree :
  Or bid me die, and I will dare
    E'en Death, to die for thee.

6. Thou art my life, my love, my heart,
    The very eyes of me :
  And hast command of every part,
    To live and die for thee.

Prevision, or Provision.

Ѓ*HAT Prince takes soone enough the Victors roome,*
  Who first provides, not to be overcome.

Obedience in Subjects.

THE Gods to Kings the *Judgement* give to sway:
The Subjects onely glory to obay.

More potent, lesse peccant.

H*E that may sin, sins least ; Leave to transgresse*
Enfeebles much the seeds of wickednesse.

Upon a maid that dyed the day
she was marryed.

THAT Morne which saw me made a Bride,
    The Ev'ning witnest that I dy'd.
Those holy lights, wherewith they guide
Unto the bed the bashfull Bride;
Serv'd, but as Tapers, for to burne,
And light my Reliques to their Urne.
This *Epitaph*, which here you see,
Supply'd the *Epithalamie.*

Upon Pink, an ill-fac'd Painter.   Epig.

TO paint the fiend, *Pink* would the Devill see ;
    And so he may, if he'll be rul'd by me :
Let but *Pink's face* i' th' Looking-glasse be showne,
And *Pink* may paint the Devill's by his owne.

Upon Brock. *Epig.*

TO cleanse his eyes, *Tom Brock* makes much adoe,
　　But not his mouth (the fouler of the two.)
A clammie Reume makes loathsome both his eyes :
His mouth, worse furr'd [6] with oathes and blasphemies.

To Meddowes.

1.　YE have been fresh and green,
　　　　Ye have been fill'd with flowers :
　　And ye the Walks have been
　　　　Where Maids have spent their houres.

2.　You have beheld, how they
　　　　With *Wicker Arks* did come
　　To kisse, and beare away
　　　　The richer Couslips home.

3.　Y'ave heard them sweetly sing,
　　　　And seen them in a Round : [7]
　　Each Virgin, like a Spring,
　　　　With Hony-succles crown'd.

4.　But now, we see, none here,
　　　　Whose silv'rie feet did tread,
　　And with dishevell'd Haire,
　　　　Adorn'd this smoother Mead.

---

[6] = fouled.　　　　　　　　[7] Dance, so called.

5. Like Unthrifts, having spent
   Your stock, and needy grown,
   Y'are left here to lament
   Your poore estates, alone.

Crosses.

THOUGH good things answer many good intents;
Crosses doe still bring forth the best events.

Miseries.

THOUGH hourely comforts from the Gods we see,
No life is yet life-proofe from miserie.

Laugh and lie down.

Y'AVE laught enough (sweet), vary now your Text;
And laugh no more; or laugh, and lie down next.

To His Houshold gods.

RISE, Houshold-gods, and let us goe;
   But whither, I my selfe not know.
First, let us dwell on rudest seas;
Next, with severest Salvages;[8]
Last, let us make our best abode,
Where humane foot, as yet, n'er trod:
Search worlds of Ice; and rather there
Dwell, then in lothèd *Devonshire.*

[8] = savages, as before.

To the Nightingale, and Robin Red-brest.

WHEN I departed am, ring thou my knell,
   Thou pittifull, and pretty *Philomel:*
And when I'm laid out for a Corse; then be
Thou *Sexton (Red-brest)* for to cover me.

To the Yew and Cypresse to grace his
Funerall.

1.   BOTH you two have
      Relation to the grave :
      And where
The *Fun'rall-Trump* sounds, you are there.

2.   I shall be made
      Ere long a fleeting shade :
      Pray come,
And doe some honour to my Tomb.

3.   Do not deny
      My last request ; for I
      Will be
Thankfull to you, or friends, for me.

I call and I call.

I CALL, I call :[9] who doe ye call?
The Maids to catch this Cowslip-ball :

[9] Looks like the catch-word of some game.

But since these Cowslips fading be,
Troth, leave the flowers, and Maids, take me.
Yet, if that neither you will doe,
Speak but the word, and Ile take you.

On a perfum'd Lady.

YOU say y'are sweet; how sho'd we know
    Whether that you be sweet or no?
From *Powders* and *Perfumes* keep free;
Then we shall smell how sweet you be.

A Nuptiall Song, or Epithalamie, on Sir Clipseby Crew *and his Lady.*[1]

1. WHAT'S that we see from far? the spring of Day
      Bloom'd from the East, or faire Injewel'd May

---

[1] See Memorial-Introduction on a MS. of which this is evidently Herrick's revised text. This was son and heir of Sir Ranulphe Crewe, Chief-Justice of the King's Bench. He was knighted 18th June, 1620. He married in 1625 Jane, d. of Sir John Pulteney, of Misterton co., Leicester, Kt. She died 2nd December, 1639, in her 50th year, and was buried in Westminster Abbey. He was also buried there 3rd Feb., 1648-9. This 'Nuptial Song' must have been composed so early as 1625. See Memorial-Introduction. With reference to various allusions in this 'Epithalamie' I quote Ben Jonson's note to his Hue and Cry after Cupid: "Here the musicians, attired in yellow with wreaths of marjoram, and veils like Hymen's priests [yellow], sung the first stave of the following Epithalamion." Marjoram, apparently from its yellow colour, seems to have been used at marriages.

Blowne out of April ; or some New-
Star fill'd with glory to our view,
　　　Reaching at heaven,
To adde a nobler Planet to the seven ?
　　Say, or doe we not descrie
Some Goddesse, in a cloud of Tiffanie [2]
　　　To move, or rather the
Emergent *Venus* from the Sea ?

2. 'Tis she ! 'tis she ! or else some more Divine
　Enlightned substance ; mark how from the Shrine
　　　Of holy Saints she paces on,
　　Treading upon *Vermilion*
　　　　And *Amber ;* Spice-
ing the Chafte-Aire with fumes of Paradise.
　　Then come on, come on, and yeeld
A savour like unto a blessed field,
　　　When the bedabled [3] Morne
Washes the golden eares of corne.

3. See where she comes ; and smell how all the street
　Breathes Vine-yards and Pomgranats : O how sweet !
　　　As a fir'd Altar, is each stone,
　　Perspiring pounded Cynamon.

[2] = fine silk, or gauze, as before.
[3] = bedewed, or wet with dew.　See Glossarial Index s. v.

The Phenix nest,
Built up of odours, burneth in her breast.
Who therein wo'd not consume
His soule to Ash-heaps in that rich perfume?
Bestroaking Fate the while
He burnes to Embers on the Pile.

4. *Himen, O Himen!* tread the sacred ground;
Shew thy white feet, and head with Marjoram
   crown'd:
   Mount up thy flames, and let thy Torch
   Display the Bridegroom in the porch,[4]
      In his desires
More towring, more disparkling [5] then thy fires:
   Shew her how his eyes do turne   [*than*
And roule about, and in their motions burne
      Their balls to Cindars: haste,
   Or else to ashes he will waste.

5. Glide by the banks of Virgins then, and passe
The Shewers [6] of Roses,[7] lucky foure-leav'd grasse:

---

[4] See Porch Verse, page 33.

[5] = throwing out sparks in different directions (i. e. by his eyes).

[6] = showers?   [7] Cf. Ben Jonson's Masque of Hymen:
   Now youths, let go your pretty arms
   The place within chants other charms.
      Whole showers of roses flow,
      And violets seem to grow,
      Strewèd in the chamber there.

The while the cloud of younglings sing,
And drown yee with a flowrie Spring :
     While some repeat
Your praise, and bless you, sprinkling you with Wheat
    While that others doe divine ;
Blest is the Bride, on whom the Sun doth shine ;
      And thousands gladly wish
   You multiply, as doth a Fish.

6. And beautious Bride we do confess y'are wise,
  In dealing forth these bashfull jealousies :
     In Lov's name do so ; and a price
     Set on your selfe, by being nice :
        But yet take heed ;
  What now you seem, be not the same indeed,
     And turne *Apostate :*[8] Love will
  Part of the way be met ; or sit stone-still.
       On then, and though you slow-
    ly go, yet, howsoever, go.

7. And now y'are enter'd ; see the Codled[9] Cook
  Runs from his *Torrid Zone*, to prie, and look,
     And blesse his dainty Mistresse : see,
     The Aged point out, This is she,

[8] So in Nicholson's *Acolastus* (1600) " this foule *apostata*."
[9] = par-boiled, i. e. overheated and steaming.

Who now must sway
The House (Love shield her) with her Yea and Nay :
And the smirk Butler thinks it
Sin, in's Nap'rie, not to express his wit ;
Each striving to devise
Some gin, wherewith to catch your eyes.

8. To bed, to bed, kind Turtles, now, and write
This the short'st day, and this the longest night ;
But yet too short for you : 'tis we,
Who count this night as long as three,
Lying alone,
Telling[10] the Clock strike Ten, Eleven, Twelve, One.
Quickly, quickly then prepare ;
And let the Young-men and the Bride-maids share
Your Garters ; and their joynts
Encircle with the Bride-grooms Points.[1]

9. By the Brides eyes, and by the teeming life
Of her green hopes, we charge ye, that no strife,
(Farther then Gentlenes tends) [2] gets place
Among ye, striving for her lace :   [*than*

[10] =counting. Cf. Milton's " Every shepherd tells his tale "
(L'Allegro, l. 67.)

[1] A tagged lace which held up the breeches.

[2] In the MS. it is ' virtue lends ' : virtue is wisely altered to ' gentlenes.' Were it not for the parenthesis one might have supposed
' tends ' to have slipped in or been left inadvertently.

O doe not fall
Foule in these noble pastimes, lest ye call
Discord in, and so divide
The youthfull Bride-groom, and the fragrant Bride :
Which Love fore-fend; but spoken
Be't to your praise, no peace was broken.

10. Strip her of Spring-time, tender-whimpring-maids,
Now *Autumne's* come, when all those flowrie aids
Of her Delayes must end; Dispose
That *Lady-smock*, that *Pansie*, and that *Rose*
Neatly apart;
But for *Prick-madam*, and for *Gentle-heart;*
And soft *Maidens-blush*,[2] the Bride
Makes holy these, all others lay aside :
Then strip her, or unto her
Let him come, who dares undo her.

11. And to enchant yee more, see every where
About the Roofe a *Syren* in a Sphere;
(As we think) singing to the dinne
Of many a warbling *Cherubin!*
O marke yee how
The soule of Nature melts in numbers: now

[3] Common bridal flowers.

See, a thousand *Cupids* flye,
To light their Tapers at the Brides bright eye.
To Bed ; or her they'l tire,
Were she an Element of fire.

12. And to your more bewitching, see, the proud
Plumpe Bed beare up, and swelling like a cloud,
Tempting the two too modest ; can
Yee see it brusle [4] like a Swan,
And you be cold
To meet it, when it woo's and seemes to fold
The Armes to hugge it ? throw, throw
Your selves into the mighty over-flow
. Of that white Pride, and Drowne
The night, with you, in floods of Downe.

13. The bed is ready, and the maze of Love
Lookes for the treaders ; every where is wove
Wit and new misterie ; read, and
Put in practise, to understand
And know each wile,
Each hieroglyphick of a kisse or smile ;

---

[4] ' Brusle ' is in one sense to ' bristle ' (the noun ' bristle ' is spelled *brustyl* in Promp. Parv.) and here signifies the bristling up of feathers which is common to birds. Its use by Herrick denotes the result of such bristling, and may be expressed by ' plumping up ' : the swan is chosen as being like the dove, sacred to Venus. 'Brustle' is still the vulgar pronunciation of ' bristle,' and to ' stick up his *brustles* ' = show his teeth, or display his temper.

And do it to the full; reach
High in your own conceipt, and some way teach
    Nature and Art, one more
  Play then they ever knew before.   [*than*

14. If needs we must for Ceremonies-sake,
Blesse a *Sack-posset ;* [5] Luck go with it ; take
    The Night-Charme quickly; you have spells,
  And magicks for to end, and hells,
      To passe ; but such
And of such Torture as no one would grutch
    To live therein for ever : Frie
And consume, and grow again to die,
    And live, and in that case,
  Love the confusion of the place.

15. But since It must be done, dispatch, and sowe
Up in a sheet your Bride, and what if so
    It be with Rock, or walles of Brasse,
  Ye Towre her up, as *Danae* was ;
    Thinke you that this,
Or hell it selfe a powerfull Bulwarke is ?
    I tell yee no ; but like a
Bold bolt of thunder he will make his way,
    And rend the cloud, and throw
  The sheet about, like flakes of snow.

    [5] Canary wine in milk.

16. All now is husht in silence ; *Midwife-moone,*
     With all her *Owle-ey'd* issue begs a boon
               Which you must grant; that's entrance; with
               Which extract, all we can call pith
                         And quintiscence
     Of Planetary bodies[6]; so commence
          All faire *Constellations*
     Looking upon yee, That two[7] Nations
                    Springing from two such Fires,
          May blaze[8] the vertue of their Sires.

               The silken Snake.

     F OR sport my *Julia* threw a Lace
          Of silke and silver at my face :
     Watchet[9] the silke was ; and did make
     A shew, as if 't 'ad been a snake :
     The suddenness did me affright ;
     But though it scar'd, it did not bite.

               Upon himselfe.

     I AM Sive-like, and can hold
          Nothing hot, or nothing cold.

---

[6] " All starry culminations drop, balm-dews to bathe thy feet."
Tennyson.

[7] Misprinted ' that, That ' : corrected by ' Two.'

[8] = blazon.   [9] = blue, as before.

Put in Love, and put in too
Jealousie, and both will through :
Put in Feare, and hope, and doubt ;
What comes in, runnes quickly out :
Put in secrecies withall,
Whatere enters, out it shall :
But if you can stop the Sive,
For mine own part, I'de as lieve
Maides sho'd say, or Virgins sing,
Herrick keeps, as holds nothing.

Upon Love.

L OVE's a thing, (as I do heare)
   Ever full of pensive feare ;
Rather then to which I'le fall,   [*than*
Trust me, I'le not like at all :
If to love I should entend,
Let my haire then stand an end :
And that terrour likewise prove,
Fatall to me in my love.
But if horrour cannot slake
Flames, which wo'd an entrance make ;
Then the next thing I desire,
Is to love, and live i' th' fire.

Reverence to Riches.

LIKE to the Income must be our expence;
Mans Fortune must be had in reverence.

Devotion makes the Deity.

WHO *formes a Godhead out of Gold or Stone,*
Makes not a God; but he that prayes to one.

To all young men that love.

I COULD wish you all, who love,
    That ye could your thoughts remove
From your Mistresses, and be,
Wisely wanton (like to me.)
I could wish you dispossest
Of that *Fiend that marres your rest;*
And with Tapers comes to fright
Your weake senses in the night.
I co'd wish, ye all, who frie
Cold as Ice, or coole as I.
But if flames best like ye, then
Much good do't ye Gentlemen.
I a merry heart will keep,
While you wring your hands and weep.

The Eyes.

'TIS a known principle in War,
  The eies be first, that conquer'd are.

No fault in women.

NO fault in women to refuse '
  The offer, which they most wo'd chuse.
No fault in women, to confesse
How tedious [1] they are in their dresse.
No fault in women, to lay on
The tincture of *Vermillion :*
And there to give the cheek a die
Of white, where nature doth deny.
No fault in women, to make show
Of largeness, when th'are nothing so :
(When true it is, the out-side swels
With inward Buckram, little else.) [2]
No fault in women, though they be
But seldome from suspition free :
No fault in womankind, at all,
If they but slip, and never fall.

---

[1] over-long.   [2] As lately with crinoline.

Upon Shark. *Epig.*

S*HARK* when he goes to any publick feast,
    Eates to ones thinking, of all there, the least.
What saves the master of the House thereby ?
When if the servants search, they may descry
In his wide Codpeece,[3] (dinner being done)
Two Napkins cram'd up, and a silver Spoòne.

Oberons *Feast.*

S*HAPCOT!* to thee the Fairy State
    I with discretion, dedicate.
Because thou prizest things that are
Curious, and un-familiar.
Take first the feast ; these dishes gone ;
Wee'l see the Fairy-Court *anon.*

A LITTLE mushroome-table spred,
    After short prayers, they set on bread ;
A Moon-parcht grain of purest wheat,
With some small glit'ring gritt, to eate
His choyce bitts with ; then in a trice
They make a feast lesse great then nice.   [*than*
But all this while his eye is serv'd,
We must not thinke his eare was sterv'd :

---

[3] See Glossarial Index s. v.

But that there was in place to stir
His Spleen, the chirring [4] Grasshopper ;
The merry Cricket, puling Flie,
The piping Gnat for minstralcy.
And now, we must imagine first,
The Elves present to quench his thirst
A pure seed-Pearle of Infant dew,
Brought and besweetned in a blew
And pregnant violet ; which done,
His kitling [5] eyes begin to runne
Quite through the table, where he spies
The hornes of paperie Butterflies :
Of which he eates, and tastes a little
Of that we call the Cuckoes spittle.[6]
A little Fuz-ball [7] pudding stands
By, yet not blessed by his hands,
That was too coorse ;[8] but then forthwith
He ventures boldly on the pith
Of sugred Rush, and eates the sagge
And well bestrutted [9] Bees sweet bagge :

[4] To ' chirre ' is to coo as a pigeon : = imitative word for chirping. Of course grasshoppers do not ' coo.'

[5] = eyes like kittens (green).

[6] The white froth which encloses the larva of the cicàda spumarià.

[7] = puff-ball or fungus.　　　　　　　　[8] = coarse.

[9] ' Sagge' means ' heavy,' so as to hang down. The meaning

Gladding his pallat with some store
Of Emits eggs ; what wo'd he more ?
But Beards of Mice, a Newt's [1] stew'd thigh,
A bloated Earewig, and a Flie ;
With the Red-capt worme, that's shut
Within the concave of a Nut,
Browne as his Tooth.　A little Moth,
Late fatned in a piece of cloth :
With withered cherries ; Mandrakes eares ;
Moles eyes ; to these, the slain-Stags teares :
The unctuous dewlaps of a Snaile ;
The broke-heart of a Nightingale
Ore-come in musicke ; [2] with a wine,
Ne're ravisht from the flattering Vine,
But gently prest from the soft side
Of the most sweet and dainty Bride,
Brought in a dainty daizie, which
He fully quaffs up to bewitch

here is—He eats the pith of the sweet ' Rush,' and, the ' Bagge ' of
the Bee.　The flight of a bee to her hive is thus graphically de-
scribed—*i.e.*, ' *sagged* down ' with the weight of her spoils.　The
word ' be-strutted ' is equally descriptive of the laden bee labouring
along, with legs stuck out, like ' struts ' or props.　See also ' strut '
in Glossarial Index.　　　　　　　　　[1] = small lizard.

[2] Reminiscence of Strada and Crashaw and John Ford.　See for
all Crashaw in Fuller Worthies' Library edn.: Vol. I. pp. 197-206.

His blood to height ; this done, commended
Grace by his Priest ; *The feast is ended.*

Event of things not in our power.

BY Time, and Counsell, doe the best we can,
Th'event is never in the power of man.

Upon her blush.

WHEN *Julia* blushes, she do's show
Cheeks like to Roses, when they blow.

Merits make the man.

OUR Honours, and our Commendations be
Due to the Merits, not Authoritie.

To Virgins.

HEARE, ye Virgins, and Ile teach, ·
What the times of old did preach.
Rosamond was in a Bower
Kept, as *Danae* in a Tower :
But yet Love (who subtile is)
Crept to that, and came to this.
Be ye lockt up like to these,
Or the rich *Hesperides ;*
Or those Babies [3] in your eyes,

[3] See Glossarial Index s. v.

In their Christall Nunneries ;
Notwithstanding Love will win,
Or else force a passage in :
And as coy be, as you can,
Gifts will get ye, or the man.

Vertue.

EACH must, in vertue, strive for to excell ;
That man lives twice, that lives the first life well.

The Bell-man.[4]

FROM noise of Scare-fires [5] rest ye free,
　From Murders *Benedicitie.*
From all mischances, that may fright
Your pleasing slumbers in the night :
Mercie secure ye all, and keep
The Goblin from ye, while ye sleep.
Past one aclock, and almost two,
My Masters all, *Good day to you.*

Bashfulnesse.

OF all our parts, the eyes expresse
　The sweetest kind of bashfulnesse.

---

[4] Cf. Milton's
　　"The Bell-man's noisy charm,
　　　To bless the doors from nightly harm." (Comus 853.)
[5] See Glossarial Index s. v.

To the most accomplisht Gentleman,
Master Edward Norgate, *Clark of the Signet to his Majesty.*[6] *Epig.*

FOR one so rarely tun'd to fit all parts ;
    For one to whom espous'd are all the Arts ;
Long have I sought for : but co'd never see
Them all concenter'd in one man, but Thee.
Thus, thou, that man art, whom the Fates conspir'd
To make but one (and that's thy selfe) admir'd.

Upon Prudence[7] Baldwin *her sicknesse.*

PRUE, my dearest Maid, is sick,
    Almost to be Lunatick :
Æsculapius ! come and bring
Means for her recovering ;
And a gallant Cock shall be
Offer'd up by Her, to Thee.

To Apollo.   *A short Hymne.*

PHŒBUS! when that I a Verse,
    Or[9] some numbers more rehearse ;
Tune my words, that they may fall,
Each way smoothly Musicall :

---

[6] Nothing more has been transmitted of him.   [7] Misprinted ' Brudence.' See Memorial-Introduction.   [8] Misprinted ' Of ' for ' Or.'

For which favour, there shall be
Swans devoted unto thee.

A *Hymne to* Bacchus.

B*ACCHUS*, let me drink no more ;
   Wild are Seas, that want a shore.
When our drinking has no stint,
There is no one pleasure in't.
I have drank up for to please
Thee, that great cup *Hercules :*
Urge no more ; and there shall be
Daffadills g'en up to Thee.

Upon Bungie.

B*UNGIE* do's fast ; looks pale ; puts Sack-cloth on ;
   Not out of Conscience, or Religion :
Or that this Yonker keeps so strict a Lent,
Fearing to break the King's Commandement :
But being poore, and knowing Flesh is deare,
He keeps not one, but many Lents i' th'yeare.

On himselfe.

H ERE down my wearyed limbs Ile lay;
   My Pilgrims staffe ; my weed [9] of gray:

[9] = dress.

My Palmers hat ; my Scallops shell ;
My Crosse ; my Cord ; and all farewell.
For having now my journey done,
(Just at the setting of the Sun)
Here I have found a Chamber fit,
(God and good friends be thankt for it)
Where if I can a lodger be
A little while from Tramplers [1] free ;
At my up-rising next, I shall,
If not requite, yet thank ye all.
Meanewhile, the *Holy-Rood* hence fright
The fouler Fiend, and evill Spright,
From scaring you or yours this night.

Casualties.

GOOD things, that come of course, far lesse doe
    please,
Then those, which come by sweet contingences. [*than*

Bribes and Gifts get all.

DEAD falls the Cause, if once the Hand be mute ;
    But let that speak, the Client gets the suit.

[1] = trampers : travelling beggars.

The End.

IF well thou hast begun, goe on fore-right ;
   It is the End that crownes us, not the Fight.

Upon a child that dyed.

HERE she lies, a pretty bud,
   Lately made of flesh and blood :
Who, as soone, fell fast asleep,
As her little eyes did peep.
Give her strewings ; but not stir
The earth, that lightly covers her.

Upon Sneape.   *Epig.*

S*NEAPE* has a face so brittle, that it breaks
   Forth into blushes, whensoere he speaks.

Content, not cates.

'TIS not the food, but the content
   That makes the Tables merriment.
Where Trouble serves the board, we eate
The Platters there, as soone as meat.
A little Pipkin with a bit
Of Mutton, or of Veale in it,
Set on my Table, (Trouble-free)
More then a Feast contenteth me.   [*than*

The Entertainment: or, Porch-verse, at the Marriage of Mr. Hen. Northly, *and the most witty Mrs.* Lettice Yard.[2]

WEELCOME ! but yet no entrance, till we blesse
    First you, then you, and both for white successe.
Profane no Porch young man and maid, for fear
Ye wrong the *Threshold-god*, that keeps peace here :
Please him, and then all good-luck will betide
You, the brisk Bridegroome, you the dainty Bride.
Do all things sweetly, and in comely wise ;
Put on your Garlands first, then Sacrifice :
That done ; when both of you have seemly fed,
We'll call on Night, to bring ye both to Bed :

[2] The Register of Dean Priory yields us this entry : " Henry Northleigh, gent, and Mris. Lettice Yard were married the 5th of Septemb. 1639. The said Henry and Lettice had a licence to solemnize their marriage from the right reverend father in God William, Lord Arch Bishopp of Canterbury, dated the xxvjth day of July, Anno Dni. 1639." Lettice Yarde was the d. of Edward Yard, of Churchton Ferrers co., Devon, by Elizabeth, d. and hcir of Walter Northcott (she remarried Barnabas Potter, Bp. of Carlisle :_ See Index of Names. She was 11 years old at the Visitation of Devon in 1620. See Memorial-Introduction.

Where being laid, all Faire signes looking on,
Fish-like, encrease then to a million :
And millions of spring-times may ye have,
Which spent, one death bring to ye both one Grave.

The good-night or Blessing.

BLESSINGS, in abundance come,
    To the Bride, and to her Groome ;
May the Bed, and this short night,
Know the fulness of delight !
Pleasures many, here attend ye,
And ere long, a Boy, Love send ye
Curld and comely, and so trimme,
Maides (in time) may ravish him.
Thus a dew of Graces fall
On ye both ; Goodnight to all.

Upon Leech.

LEECH boasts, he has a Pill, that can alone,
    With speed give sick men their salvation :
'Tis strange, his Father long time has been ill,
And credits Physick, yet not trusts his Pill :
And why? he knowes he must of Cure despaire,
Who makes the slie Physitian his Heire.

To Daffadills.

1. FAIRE Daffadills, we weep to see
 You haste away so soone:
As yet the early-rising Sun
 Has not attain'd his Noone.
  Stay, stay,
 Untill the hasting day
  Has run
 But to the Even-song;
And, having pray'd together, we
 Will go with you along.

2. We have short time to stay, as you,
 We have as short a Spring;
As quick a growth to meet Decay,
 As you, or any thing.
  We die,
 As your hours doe, and drie
  Away,
 Like to the Summers raine;
Or as the pearles of Mornings dew
 Ne'r to be found againe.

To a Maid.

YOU say, you love me; that I thus must prove;
If that you lye, then I will sweare you love.

Upon a Lady that dyed in child-bed, and left a daughter behind her.

AS Gilly flowers do but stay
    To blow, and seed, and so away ;
So you sweet Lady (sweet as May)
The gardens-glory liv'd a while,
To lend the world your scent and smile.
But when your own faire print was set
Once in a Virgin *Flosculet*,[3]
(Sweet as your selfe, and newly blown)
To give that life, resign'd your own :
But so, as still the mothers power
Lives in the pretty Lady-flower.

A New yeares gift sent to Sir Simeon Steward.[4]

NO news of Navies burnt at Seas ;
    No noise of late spawn'd *Tittyries :*[5]

---

[3] This is a double diminutive (of flos: 1st dimin. flosculus)—a tiny little flower, not as in Halliwell—a parterre, as shown (1) by its being applied to the babe (2) as the babe in last line is called a ' baby-flower.'

[4] See Memorial-Introduction.

[5] = titularies, titles ? Or is it a misprint for Titlyries ? The ' newes of Navies burnt at Seas ' being undated, leaves us at sea.

No closset plot, or open vent,
That frights men with a Parliament :
No new devise, or late-found trick,
To read by th' Starres, the Kingdoms sick :
No ginne to catch the State, or wring
The free-born Nosthrill of the King,
We send to you ; but here a jolly
Verse crown'd with *Yvie*, and with *Holly :*
That tels of Winters Tales and Mirth,
That Milk-Maids make about the hearth,
Of Christmas sports, the *Wassell-boule,*[6]
That tost up, after *Fox-i'th'hole :* [7]
Of *Blind-man-buffe*, and of the care
That young men have to shooe the *Mare :* [8]
Of Twelf-tide Cakes, of Pease, and Beanes
Wherewith ye make those merry Sceanes,
Whenas ye chuse your King and Queen,
And cry out, *Hey, for our town green.*
Of Ash-heapes, in the which ye use
Husbands and Wives by streakes to chuse : [9]

[6] See Glossarial Index s. v.

[7] An old English game : boys hopped on one leg and beat one another with gloves or pieces of leather tied at the end of strings.

[8] Or shoe the wild mare—a game.

[9] Folk-lore = ash-heapes. This divination to discover husbands or wives is generally used on St. Agnes' Eve. See Strutt s. v.

Of crackling Laurell, which fore-sounds,
A Plentious harvest to your grounds :
Of these, and such like things, for shift,
We send in stead of New-yeares gift.
Read then, and when your faces shine
With bucksome meat and capring Wine :
Remember us in Cups full crown'd,
And let our Citie-health go round,
Quite through the young maids and the men,
To the ninth number, if not tenne;
Untill the firèd Chesnuts leape
For joy, to see the fruits ye reape,[1]
From the plumpe Challice, and the Cup,
That tempts till it be tossèd up :
Then as ye sit about your embers,
Call not to mind those fled Decembers ;
But think on these, that are t'appeare,
As Daughters to the instant [2] yeare :
Sit crown'd with Rose-buds, and carouse,
Till *Liber Pater* [3] twirles the house
About your eares ; and lay upon
The yeare (your cares) that's fled and gon.

---

[1] Further Folk-lore.
[2] = present.   See Glossarial Index s. v.   [3] = Bacchus ?

And let the russet Swaines the Plough
And Harrow hang up resting now ;
And to the Bag-pipe [4] all addresse ;
Till sleep takes place of wearinesse.
And thus, throughout, with Christmas playes
Frolick the full twelve Holy-dayes.

Mattens, or morning Prayer.

WHEN with the Virgin morning thou do'st rise,
    Crossing thy selfe ; come thus to sacrifice :
First wash thy heart in innocence, then bring
Pure hands, pure habits, pure, pure every thing.
Next to the Altar humbly kneele, and thence,
Give up thy soule in clouds of frankinsence.
Thy golden Censors fill'd with odours sweet,
Shall make thy actions with their ends to meet.

Evensong.

BEGINNE with *Jove* ;[5] then is the worke halfe done ;
    And runnes most smoothly, when tis well begunne.
Jove's is the first and last : the Morn's his due,
The midst is thine ; but *Joves* the Evening too ;

---

[4] Not at all peculiar to Scotland, as vulgarly supposed.
[5] Dimidium facti, qui cœpit, habet, &c.   Horace : Epistle i. 2. 40.

As sure a *Mattins* do's to him belong,
So sure he layes claime to the *Evensong*.

The Bracelet to Julia.

WHY I tye about thy wrist,
　　Julia, this my silken twist;
For what other reason is't,
But to shew thee how in part,
Thou my pretty Captive art?
But thy Bondslave is my heart:
'Tis but silke that bindeth thee,
Knap [6] the thread, and thou art free:
But 'tis otherwise with me;
I am bound, and fast bound so,
That from thee I cannot go,
If I co'd, I wo'd not so.

The Christian Militant.

A MAN prepar'd against all ills to come,
　　That dares to dead the fire of martirdome:
That sleeps at home; and sayling there at ease,
Feares not the fierce sedition of the Seas:

---

[6] = snap. So in Prayer Book version of Psalm xlvi. v. 9, " and knappeth the spear in sunder."

That's counter-proofe against the Farms mis-haps,
Undreadfull too of courtly thunderclaps :
That weares one face (like heaven) and never showes
A change, when Fortune either comes, or goes :[7]
That keepes his own strong guard, in the despight
Of what can hurt by day, or harme by night :
That takes and re-delivers every stroake
Of Chance (as made up all of rock, and oake :)
That sighs at others death ; smiles at his own
Most dire and horrid crucifixion.
Who for true glory suffers thus ; we grant
Him to be here our *Christian militant.*

A short Hymne to Larr.[8]

THOUGH I cannot give thee fires
    Glit'ring to my free desires :
These accept, and Ile be free,
Offering *Poppy* unto thee.

Another to Neptune.

MIGHTY *Neptune,* may it please
    Thee, the *Rector*[9] of the Seas,

---

[7] Horace, throughout.   [8] See Glossarial Index s. v.
[9] = regent or ruler.

That my Barque may safely runne
Through thy watrie-region ;
And a *Tunnie-fish* shall be
Offer'd up, with thanks to thee.

Upon Greedy. *Epig.*

AN old, old widow *Greedy* needs wo'd wed,
     Not for affection to her, or her Bed ;
But in regard, 'twas often said, this old
Woman wo'd bring him more then co'd be told,
He tooke her; now the jest in this appeares,   [*than*
So old she was, that none co'd tell her yeares.

His embalming to Julia.

FOR my embalming, *Julia*, do but this,
     Give thou my lips but their supreamest kiss :
Or else trans-fuse thy breath into the chest,
Where my small reliques must for ever rest :
That breath the *Balm*, the *myrrh*, the *Nard* shal be,
To give an *incorruption* unto me.

Gold, before Goodnesse.

HOW rich a man is, all desire to know ;
     But none enquires if good he be, or no.

The Kisse.   *A Dialogue.*

1. AMONG thy Fancies, tell me this,
  What is the thing we call a kisse ?
2. I shall resolve ye, what it is.

  It is a creature born and bred
  Between the lips, (all cherrie-red,)
  By love and warme desires fed,
Chor. And makes more soft the Bridall Bed.

2. It is an active flame, that flies,
  First, to the Babies [1] of the eyes ;
  And charmes them there with lullabies ;
Chor. And stils the Bride too, when she cries.

2. Then to the chin, the cheek, the eare,
  It frisks, and flyes, now here, now there,
  'Tis now farre off, and then tis nere ;
Chor. And here, and there, and every where.

1. Ha's it a speaking virtue ?   2. Yes.
1. How speaks it, say ?   2. Do you but this,
  Part your joyn'd lips, then speaks your kisse ;
Chor. And this Loves sweetest language is.

[1] See Glossarial Index s. v.

1. Has it a body? 2. I, and wings,   [*ay*
    With thousand rare encolourings :
    And as it flyes, it gently sings,
Chor. Love, honie yeelds ; but never stings.

The admonition.

SEEST thou those *Diamonds* which she weares
        In that rich Carkanet ; [2]
Or those on her dishevel'd haires,
        Faire Pearles in order set ?
Beleeve young man all those were teares
        By wretched Wooers sent,
In mournfull *Hyacinths* and *Rue*,
        That figure discontent ;
Which when not warmèd by her view,
        By cold neglect, each one,
Congeal'd to Pearle and stone ;
        Which precious spoiles upon her,
        She weares as trophees of her honour.
Ah then consider ! What all this implies ;
She that will weare thy teares, wo'd weare thine eyes.

---

[2] *Ibid.*

To his honoured kinsman *Sir* William Soame.[3] *Epig.*

I CAN but name thee, and methinks I call
All that have been, or are canonicall
For love and bountie, to come neare, and see,
Their many vertues volum'd up in thee ;
In thee Brave Man ! Whose incorrupted fame,
Casts forth a light like to a Virgin flame :
And as it shines, it throwes a scent about,
As when a Rain-bow in perfumes goes out.
So vanish hence, but leave a name, as sweet,
As *Benjamin*, and *Storax*,[4] when they meet.

On himselfe.

ASKE me, why I do not sing
To the tension of the string,
As I did, not long ago,
When my numbers full did flow ?

---

[3] The 2nd son of Sir Stephen Soame, Lord Mayor of London in 1598. He was successively sheriff and alderman of London, and M. P. for the city in 1640, but was subsequently excluded from the House for his Royalism. He died 1st Jan., 1670-1, aged 88, and was buried at Throcking co., Herts.

[4] Benjamin, the favourite youngest son of the Patriarch : Storax = balsam of liquid amber orientale.

Griefe (ay me !) hath struck my Lute,
And my tongue at one time mute.

To Larr.[5]

NO more shall I, since I am driven hence,
      Devote to thee my graines of Fankinsence :
No more shall I from mantle-trees [6] hang downe,
To honour thee, my little Parsly crown :
No more shall I (I feare me) to thee bring
My chives [7] of Garlick for an offering :
No more shall I, from henceforth, heare a quire
Of merry Crickets by my Country fire.
Go where I will, thou luckie *Larr* stay here,
Warme by a glit'ring chimnie all the yeare.

The departure of the good Demon.

WHAT can I do in Poetry,
      Now the good Spirit's gone from me ?
Why nothing now, but lonely sit,
And over-read what I have writ.

[5] See Glossarial Index s. v.
[6] = piece of timber laid across head of chimney.
[7] See Glossarial Index s. v.

Clemency.

FOR punishment in warre, it will suffice,
    If the chiefe author of the faction dyes ;
Let but few smart, but strike a feare through all :
Where the fault springs, there let the judgement fall.

His age, dedicated to his peculiar friend, M. John
    Wickes, *under the name of* Posthumus.[8]

1.   AH *Posthumus !* Our yeares hence flye,
      And leave no sound ; nor piety,
        Or prayers, or vow
    Can keepe the wrinkle from the brow :
        But we must on,
    As Fate do's lead or draw us ; none,
    None, *Posthumus,* co'd ere decline
    The doome of cruell *Proserpine.*

2. The pleasing wife, the house, the ground
    Must all be left, no one plant found

---

[8] This was John Weekes, who is recorded by Wood in his
"Fasti" (s. n.) He was a wit and popular preacher. He suffered
as a Royalist. The Ode is skilfully imitative in first part of Horace.
See Odes B. 2. 14 : B. 4. 7 : B. 2. 18 (Baiae), but he probably takes
' brave ' from the ' amoenae' of Ep. B. 1. 1.

To follow thee,
Save only the *Curst-Cipresse* tree :
A merry mind
Looks forward, scornes what's left behind :
Let's live, my *Wickes*, then, while we may,
And here enjoy our Holiday.

3. W'ave seen the past-best Times, and these
Will nere return, we see the Seas,
    And Moons to wain ;
But they fill up their Ebbs again :
    But vanisht, man
Like to a Lilly-lost, nere can,
Nere can repullulate,[9] or bring
His dayes to see a second Spring.

4. But on we must, and thither tend,
Where *Anchus* and rich *Tullus* blend [1]
    Their sacred seed :
Thus has *Infernall Jove* decreed ;
    We must be made,
Ere long, a song, ere long, a shade.
Why then, since life to us is short,
Let's make it full up, by our sport.

[9] = to bud or sprout, or become young again.
[1] See Odes, as before.

5. Crown we our Heads with Roses then,
   And 'noint with *Tïrian Balme;* for when
          We two are dead,
   The world with us is burièd.
            Then live we free,
   As is the Air, and let us be
   Our own fair wind, and mark each one
   Day with the white and Luckie stone.[2]

6. We are not poore ; although we have
   No roofs of Cedar, nor our brave
         Baiæ, nor keep
   Account of such a flock of sheep ;
         Nor Bullocks fed
   To lard the shambles : Barbels[3] bred
   To kisse our hands, nor do we wish
   For *Pollio's* Lampries in our dish.

7. If we can meet, and so conferre,
   Both by a shining Salt-seller ;
         And have our Roofe,
   Although not archt, yet weather-proofe,

---

[2] Revelation, c. ii. 17.   [3] = river fish.

And seeling [4] free,
From that cheape *Candle baudery* : [5]
We'le eate our Beane with that full mirth
As we were Lords of all the earth.

8. Well then, on what Seas we are tost,
Our comfort is, we can't be lost.
            Let the winds drive
Our Barke ; yet she will keepe alive
            Amidst the deepes ;
'Tis constancy (my *Wickes*) which keepes
The Pinnace up ; which though she erres [6]
I'th' Seas, she saves her passengers.

9. Say, we must part (sweet mercy blesse,
Us both i'th' Sea, Camp, Wildernesse)
            Can we so farre
Stray, to become lesse circular,[7]
            Then we are now ?   [*than*
No, no, that selfe same heart, that vow,

---

[4] =ceiling.   [5] Obscene words and figures made with candle-smoke, not unfrequently met with in the habitations of the vulgar.

[6] Wanders.

[7] Is this the Horatian "totus, teres, atque rotundus"? (S. 2. 7. 86) i. e. as implying perfection. It is a not uncommon expression of the time for perfection, even as the circle was held the most perfect figure. Cf. Donne.

Which made us one, shall ne'r undoe ;
Or ravell so, to make us two.

10. Live in thy peace ; as for my selfe,
When I am bruisèd on the Shelfe
       Of Time, and show
My locks behung with frost and snow :
       When with the reume,
The cough, the ptisick,[8] I consume
Unto an almost nothing ; then,
The Ages fled, Ile call agen :

11. And with a teare compare these last
Lame, and bad times, with those are past,
       While *Baucis* by,[9]
My old leane wife, shall kisse it dry :
       And so we'l sit
By'th'fire, foretelling snow and slit,[10]
And weather by our aches,[1] grown
Now old enough to be our own

12. True Calenders, as Pusses eare
Washt o'rs, to tell what change is neare :[2]

---

[8] Pthsis = consumptive disease ?
[9] = an old woman (Persius 4. 21).   [10] = sleet.
[1] Two syllables—as Kemble pronounced it in Shakespeare.
[2] Weather lore.

Then to asswage
The gripings of the chine [3] by age ;
I'le call my young
Iülus to sing such a song
I made upon my *Julia's* brest ;
And of her blush at such a feast.

13. Then shall he read that flowre of mine
Enclos'd within a christall shrine : [4]
A Primrose next ;
A piece, then of a higher text :
For to beget
In me a more transcendant heate,
Then that insinuating fire. [5]   [*than*
Which crept into each agèd Sire ;

14. When the faire *Hellen*, from her eyes,
Shot forth her loving Sorceries :
At which I'le reare
Mine agèd limbs above my chaire :
And hearing it,
Flutter and crow, as in a fit
Of fresh concupiscence, and cry,
No lust theres like to Poetry.

---

[3] = spine or back-bone.   [4] See Memorial-Introduction.
[5] Reference (but inaccurate) to Iliad III.

15. Thus frantick-crazie man (God wot)
 Ile call to mind things half forgot :
  And oft between,
 Repeat the Times that I have seen !
  Thus ripe with tears,
 And twisting my *Iülus* hairs ;
 Doting, Ile weep and say (In Truth)
 Baucis, these were my sins of youth.

16. Then next Ile cause my hopefull Lad
 (If a wild Apple can be had)
  To crown the Hearth,
 (*Larr*[6] thus conspiring with our mirth)
  Then to infuse
 Our browner Ale into the cruse :
 Which sweetly spic't, we'l first carouse
 Unto the *Genius* of the house.

17. Then the next health to friends of mine
 (Loving the brave *Burgundian wine*)
  High sons of Pith,[7]
 Whose fortunes I have frolickt with :

---

[6] See Glossarial Index s. v.

[7] = sons of strength ; so used because strong lusty men were supposed to have a well-pith'd or well-marrowed back-bone. See Glossarial Index s. v.

Such as co'd well
Bear up the Magick bough, and spel :
And dancing 'bout the Mystick *Thyrse,*
Give up the just applause to verse :

18. To those, and then agen to thee
    We'l drink, my *Wickes,* untill we be
                        Plump as the cherry,
    Though not so fresh, yet full as merry
                        As the crickit ;
    The untam'd Heifer, or the Pricket,[8]
    Untill our tongues shall tell our ears,
    W'are younger by a score of years.

19. Thus, till we see the fire lesse shine
    From th' embers then the kitlings eyne,[9]   [*than*
                        We'l still sit up,
    Sphering about the wassail cup,
                        To all those times,
    Which gave me honour for my Rhimes :
    The cole once spent, we'l then to bed,
    Farre more then night-bewearièd.   [*than*

---

[8] = a 2-year old male deer.   [9] See Glossarial Index s. v.

A short hymne to Venus.

GODDESSE, I do love a Girle
    Rubie-lipt, and tooth'd with *Pearl :*
If so be, I may but prove
Luckie in this Maide I love :
I will promise there shall be
Mirtles offer'd up to Thee.

To a Gentlewoman on just dealing.

TRUE to your self, and sheets, you'l have me
    swear,
You shall ; if righteous dealing I find there. ·
Do not you fall through frailty ; Ile be sure
To keep my Bond still free from forfeiture.

The hand and tongue.

TWO parts of us successively command ;
    The tongue in peace ; but then in warre the
    hand.

Upon a delaying Lady.

  1. COME come away,
      Or let me go ;
    Must I here stay
    Because y'are slow ;
    And will continue so ?
    Troth, Lady, no.

2. I scorne to be
   A slave to state :
   And since I'm free,
   I will not wait,
   Henceforth at such a rate,
   For needy Fate.

3. If you desire
   My spark sho'd glow,
   The peeping fire
   You must blow ;
   Or I shall quickly grow,
   To Frost, or Snow.

To the Lady Mary Villars, *Governesse to the Princesse* Henretta.[1]

WHEN I of *Villars* doe but heare the name,
      It calls to mind, that mighty *Buckingham*,
Who was your brave exalted Uncle here,
(Binding the wheele of Fortune to his Sphere)
Who spurn'd at Envie; and co'd bring, with ease,
An end to all his stately purposes.
For his love then, whose sacred Reliques show
Their Resurrection, and their growth in you :

[1] See Memorial-Introduction.

And for my sake, who ever did prefer
You, above all Those *Sweets* of *Westminster* :[2]
Permit my Book to have a free accesse
To kisse your hand, most Dainty Governesse.

Upon his Julia.

WILL ye heare, what I can say
    Briefly of my *Julia ?*
Black and rowling is her eye,
Double chinn'd, and forehead high :
Lips she has, all Rubie red,
Cheeks like Creame Enclaritèd :[3]
And a nose that is the grace
And *Proscenium*[4] of her face.
So that we may guesse by these,
The other parts will richly please.

To Flowers.

IN time of life, I grac't ye with my Verse ;
    Doe now your flowrie honours to my Herse.
You shall not languish, trust me : Virgins here
Weeping, shall make ye flourish all the yeere.

---

[2] = other beauties of Westminster and Whitehall.

[3] = made ruddy with claret or strawberries. See Glossarial Index
s. v.   [4] = front of the stage before the curtain ; but Herrick was
evidently thinking of the Proscenium of the classic theatre.

To my ill Reader.

THOU say'st my lines are hard ;
  And I the truth will tell ;
They are both hard, and marr'd,
  If thou not read'st them well.

The Power in the people.

LET Kings Command, and doe the best they may,
  The saucie Subjects still will beare the sway.

A Hymne to Venus, *and* Cupid.

SEA-BORN Goddesse, let me be,
  By thy sonne thus grac't, and thee ;
That whenere I wooe, I find
Virgins coy, but not unkind.
Let me when I kisse a maid,
Taste her lips, so over-laid
With Loves-sirrop ; that I may,
In your Temple, when I pray,
Kisse the Altar, and confess
Ther's in love, no bitterness.

On Julia's *Picture.*

HOW am I ravisht ! when I do but see,
    The Painters art in thy *Sciography ?* [5]
If so, how much more shall I dote thereon,
When once he gives it incarnation?

Her Bed.

SEE'ST thou that Cloud as silver cleare,
    Plump, soft, & swelling everywhere ?
'Tis *Julia's* Bed, and she sleeps there.

Her Legs.

FAIN would I kiss my *Julia's* dainty Leg,
    Which is as white and hair-less [6] as an egge.

Upon her Almes.

SEE how the poore do waiting stand,
    For the expansion of thy hand.
A wafer [7] Dol'd by thee, will swell
Thousands to feed by miracle.

---

[5] Properly sciagraphy = drawing in shaded outline.
[6] The proverb "to shave an egg." See Glossarial Index s. v.
[7] = thin biscuit, as in Communion bread.

Rewards.

STILL to our gains our chief respect is had ;
Reward it is, that makes us good or bad.

Nothing new.

NOTHING is New : we walk where others went
Ther's no vice now, but has his president.[8]

The Rainbow.

LOOK, how the *Rainbow* doth appeare
But in one onely *Hemisphere :*
So likewise after our disseace,
No more is seen the Arch of Peace.
That Cov'nant's here ; The under-bow,
That nothing shoots, but war and woe.

The meddow verse or Aniversary to Mistris Bridget Lowman.[9]

COME with the Spring-time forth Fair Maid, and
be
This year again, the *medows Deity.*
Yet ere ye enter, give us leave to set
Upon your Head this flowry Coronet :

[8] = precedent. [9] Not known, apparently.

To·make this neat distinction from the rest ;
You are the Prime, and Princesse of the Feast :
To which, with silver feet lead you the way,
While sweet-breath Nimphs, attend on you this Day.
This is your houre ; and best you may command,
Since you are Lady of this Fairie land.
Full mirth wait on you ; and such'mirth as shall
Cherrish the cheek, but make none blush at all.

The parting verse, the feast there ended.

LOTH to depart, but yet at last, each one
    Back must now go to's habitation :
Not knowing thus much, when we once do sever,
Whether or no, that we shall meet here ever.
As for myself, since time a thousand cares
And griefs hath fil'de [1] upon my silver hairs ;
'Tis to be doubted whether I next yeer,
Or no, shall give ye a re-meeting here.
If die I must, then my last vow shall be,
You'l with a tear or two, remember me,
Your sometime Poet ; but if fates do give
Me longer date, and more fresh Springs to live :

---

[1] = defiled.

Oft as your field, shall her old age renew,
Herrick shall make the meddow-verse [2] for you.

Upon Judith. *Epig.*

J *UDITH* has cast her old-skin, and got new;
And walks fresh varnisht to the publick view.
Foule *Judith* was ; and foule she will be known,
For all this fair *Transfiguration.*

Long and lazie.

T HAT was the Proverb. Let my mistresse be
Lasie to others, but be long to me.

Upon Ralph. *Epig.*

C URSE not the mice, no grist of thine they eat :
But curse thy children, they consume thy wheat.

To the right honourable, Philip, *Earle of Pembroke, and Montgomerie.* [3]

H OW dull and dead are books, that cannot show
A *Prince* of *Pembroke,* and that *Pembroke,* [4] you !

[2] = See Glossarial Index.

[3] Philip Herbert, 4th Earl of Pembroke, succeeded to the title on the death of his brother William, 10th April, 1630, being already Earl of Montgomery. He was Lord-Chamberlain of the household to King Charles I., and Chancellor of the University of Oxford. He died in 1655.

[4] He may allude to the little ancient principalities of the Welsh.

You, who are High born, and a Lord no lesse
Free by your fate, then Fortune's mightinesse, [*than*
Who hug our Poems (Honourd Sir) and then
The paper gild, and Laureat the pen.
Nor suffer you the Poets to sit cold,
But warm their wits, and turn their lines to gold.
Others there be, who righteously will swear
Those smooth-pac't Numbers, amble every where ;
And these brave Measures go a stately trot ;
Love those, like these ; regard, reward them not.
But you, my Lord, are One, whose hand along
Goes with your mouth, or do's outrun your tongue ;
Paying before you praise ; and cockring ⁵ wit,
Give both the Gold and Garland unto it.

An hymne to Juno.

STATELY Goddesse, do thou please,
    Who art chief at marriages,
But to dresse the Bridall-Bed,
When my Love and I shall wed :
And a *Peacock* proud shall be
Offerd up by us, to thee.

---

⁵ =and [those] pampering [my] wit.

Upon Mease.   *Epig.*

M*EASE* brags of Pullets which he eats : but
     Mease
Ne'r yet set tooth in stump, or rump of these.

Upon Sapho, *sweetly playing, and
     sweetly singing.*

W HEN thou do'st play, and sweetly sing,
     Whether it be the voice or string,
Or both of them, that do agree
Thus to en-trance and ravish me :
This, this I know, I'm oft struck mute ;
And dye away upon thy Lute.

Upon Paske *a Draper.*

P*ASKE*, though his debt be due upon the day
     Demands no money by a craving way;
For why sayes he, all debts and their arreares,
Have reference to the shoulders, not the eares.[6]

Chop-Cherry.[7]

1. T HOU gav'st me leave to kisse ;
V   Thou gav'st me leave to wooe ;

---

[6] Query—Is the meaning that he does not ask for a debt over-
due, but sends a shoulder-tapper to arrest the debtor?

[7] A child-sport.

Thou mad'st me thinke by this,
    And that, thou lov'dst me too.

2. But I shall ne'r forget,
    How for to make thee merry;
Thou mad'st me chop, but yet,
    Another snapt the Cherry.

*To the most learned, wise, and Arch-Anti-
quary, M. John Selden.*[8]

I WHO have favour'd many, come to be
    Grac't (now at last) or glorifi'd by thee.
Loe, I, the Lyrick Prophet, who have set
On many a head the Delphick Coronet,
Come unto thee for Laurell, having spent,
My wreaths on those, who little gave or lent.
Give me the *Daphne*, that the world may know it,
Whom they neglected, thou hast crown'd a Poet.
A City here of *Heroes* I have made,
Upon the rock, whose firm foundation laid,
Shall never shrink, where making thine abode,
Live thou a *Selden*, that's a Demi-god.

[8] The illustrious Thinker: born 1584: died 1654.

Upon himself.

THOU shalt not All die ;[9] for while Love's fire
　　shines
Upon his Altar, men shall read thy lines ;
And learn'd Musicians shall to honour *Herricks*
Fame, and his Name, both set, and sing his Lyricks.

Upon wrinkles.

WRINKLES no more are, or no lesse,
　　Then beauty turn'd to sowernesse.　[*than*

Upon Prigg.

P*RIGG*, when he comes to houses, oft doth use
　　(Rather then fail) to steal from thence old shoes :
Sound or unsound, or be they or [1] rent or whole,
Prigg bears away the body and the sole.

Upon Moon.

MOON is an Usurer, whose gain,
　　Seldome or never, knows a wain,
Onely Moons conscience, we confesse,
That ebs from pittie lesse and lesse.

---

[9] "Non omnis moriar." Horace.　See of Lyricks ' set and sung '
in Memorial-Introduction.　　　　　　[1] I insert ' or ' (*bis*)

Pray and prosper.

FIRST offer Incense, then thy field and meads
    Shall smile and smell the better by thy beads.
The spangling Dew dreg'd [2] o're the grasse shall be
Turn'd all to Mell,[3] and Manna there for thee.
Butter of *Amber*,[4] *Cream*, and *Wine*, and *Oile*
Shall run, as rivers, all throughout thy soyl.
Wod'st thou to sincere [5]-silver turn thy mold ?
Pray once, twice pray ; and turn thy ground to gold.

His Lachrimæ or Mirth, turn'd
to mourning.

1. CALL me no more,
        As heretofore,
The musick of a Feast ;
        Since now (alas)
        The mirth, that was
In me, is dead or ceast.

2. Before I went
        To banishment
Into the loathèd West ;

---

[2] = dredged, i. e., sprinkled.   [3] = honey.
[4] = as yellow as amber, but with an allusion also to ambergris.
[5] = pure.

I co'd rehearse
A Lyrick verse,
And speak it with the best.

3. But time (Ai me)
Has laid, I see,
My Organ fast asleep ;
And turn'd my voice
Into the noise
Of those that sit and weep.

Upon Shift.

S*HIFT* now has cast his clothes : got all things
  new ;
Save but his hat,[6] and that he cannot mew.[7]

Upon Cuts.

I F wounds in clothes, *Cuts* calls his rags, 'tis cleere,
His linings are the matter running there.

Gain and Gettings.

W HEN others gain much by the present cast,
The coblers getting time, is at the Last.

---

[6] = his hair.   [7] = moult, i. e. the word which describes the
annual casting and renewing of feathers.

To the most fair and lovely Mistris,
Anne Soame, *now Lady* Abdie.[8]

SO smell those odours that do rise
    From out the wealthy spiceries :
So smels the flowre of *blooming Clove ;*
Or *Roses* smother'd in the stove :
So smells the Aire of spicèd Wine ;
Or *Essences* of *Jessimine :*
So smells the Breath about the hives,
When well the work of hony thrives ;
And all the *busie Factours* [9] come
Laden with wax and hony home :
So smell those neat and woven Bowers,
All over-archt with *Oringe flowers,*
And *Almond blossoms,* that do mix
To make rich these *Aromatikes :*
So smell those bracelets, and those bands
Of *Amber* chaf't between the hands,
When thus enkindled they transpire
A noble perfume from the fire.

[8] Anne, eldest d. of Sir Thomas Soane, of London, Kt., and 2nd
wife of Sir Thomas Abdy, first baronet of Felix Hall, Essex (his first
wife died 6th April, 1645.) She died 19th June, 1679. She was
ancestress of the line of baronets which became extinct in 1868.
  [9] = workers, agents.

The wine of cherries, and to these,
The cooling breath of Respasses ;[1]
The smell of mornings milk, and cream ;
Butter of *Cowslips* mixt with them ;
Of rosted warden,[2] or bak'd peare,
These are not to be reckon'd here ;
Whenas the meanest part of her,
Smells like the maiden-Pomander.
Thus sweet she smells, or what can be
More lik'd by her, or lov'd by mee.

Upon his Kinswoman Mistris Elizabeth Herrick.[3]

SWEET virgin, that I do not set
  The pillars up of weeping *Jet*,
Or mournfull *Marble;* let thy shade
Not wrathfull seem, or fright the Maide,
Who hither at her wonted howers
Shall come to strew thy earth with flowers.
No, know (Blest Maide) when there's not one
Remainder left of Brasse or stone,
Thy living Epitaph shall be,
Though lost in them, yet found in me.

---

[1] Raspises: sing. raspis (Cotgrave), i. e. = raspberries.
[2] = large pear : *pyrum volemum.* It also, in 'warden pies,' meant a somewhat insipid dish, which was made 'tasty' by nutmeg, cloves, &c.   [3] See Memorial-Introduction.

Dear, in thy *bed of Roses*, then,
Till this world shall dissolve as men,
Sleep, while we hide thee from the light,
Drawing thy curtains round : *Good night.*

A Panegerick to Sir Lewis Pemberton.[4]

TILL I shall come again, let this suffice,
    I send my salt, my sacrifice
To Thee, thy Lady, younglings, and as farre
    As to thy *Genius* and thy *Larre;*[5]
To the worn Threshold, Porch, Hall, Parlour, Kitchin,
    The fat-fed smoking Temple, which in
The wholsome savour of thy mighty Chines
    Invites to supper him who dines,
Where laden spits, warp't[6] with large Ribbs of Beefe,
    Not represent, but give reliefe
To the lanke-Stranger, and the sowre Swain ;
    Where both may feed, and come againe :
For no black-bearded *Vigil*[7] from thy doore
    Beats with a button'd-staffe[8] the poore :

---

[4] He was of Rushden co., Northampton, and died about 1641 (his Will proved in that year). One of his daughters married Sir Walter Littleton, Chancellor of Lichfield.

[5] See Glossarial Index s. v.   [6] =bent.

[7] =Latin : a watchman or guard.   [8] =a staff with a knob as a sign of office. See Glossarial Index s. v.

But from thy warm-love-hatching gates each may
    Take friendly morsels, and there stay
To Sun his thin-clad members, if he likes,
    For thou no Porter keep'st who strikes.
No commer to thy Roofe his *Guest-rite* wants ;
    Or staying there, is scourg'd with taunts
Of some rough Groom, who (yirkt [9] with Corns) sayes,
    Sir,
    Y'ave dipt too long i'th Vinegar ;
And with our Broth and bread, and bits ; Sir, friend,
    Y'ave farèd well, pray make an end ;
Two dayes y'ave larded here ; a third, yee know,
    Makes guests and fish smell strong ; pray go
You to some other chimney, and there take
    Essay [1] of other giblets ;[2] make
You [3] merry at anothers hearth ; y'are here
    Welcome as thunder to our beere :[4]
Manners knowes distance, and a man unrude [5]
    Wo'd soon recoile, and not intrude

---

[9] 'Yirk' being same as 'yerk' is stronger than 'irk,' and is=
struck with, afflicted with.   [1] =trial.

[2] This is of course put—a part for the whole—for dainty bits, but
is a particular part. Also=the offals, i. e. insides, as liver, heart,
gizzard, ' rits,' (entrails scraped and cleaned)—the neck, smaller
joints of the wings, &c., made usually into pies,—all taken off when
the poultry are prepared for the table.   [3] I fill in ' you.'

[4] Thunder is supposed to sour ' beer.'   [5] =not rude.

His Stomach to a second Meale.   No, no,
     Thy house, well fed and taught, can show
No such crab'd vizard :[6] Thou hast learnt thy Train,
     With heart and hand to entertain :
And by the Armes-full (with a Brest unhid)
     As the old Race of mankind did,
When eithers heart, and either's hand did strive
     To be the nearer Relative :
Thou do'st redeeme those times ; and what was lost
     Of antient honesty, may boast
It keeps a growth in thee ; and so will runne
     A course in thy Fames-pledge, *thy Sonne.*
Thus, like a *Roman Tribune,* thou thy gate
     Early setts ope to feast, and late :
Keeping no *currish Waiter* to affright,
     With blasting eye, the appetite,
Which fain would waste upon thy Cates, but that
     The *Trencher-creature* marketh what
Best and more suppling piece he cuts, and by
     Some private pinch tels danger's nie,
A hand too desp'rate, or a knife that bites
     Skin-deepe into the Porke, or lights
Upon some part of Kid, as if mistooke,
     When check'd by the Butlers look.
No, no, thy bread, thy wine, thy jocund Beere

[6] = mask, or face as ill-looking as a mask.

Is not reserv'd for *Trebius*[7] here,
But all, who at thy table seated are,
    Find equall freedome, equall fare ;
And thou, like to that *Hospitable God*,
    Jove, joy'st when guests make their abode
To eate thy Bullocks thighs, thy Veales, thy fat
    Weathers, and never grudgèd at.
The *Phesant, Partridge, Gotwit*,[8] *Reeve*,[9] *Ruffe*,[1] *Raile*,[2]
    The *Cock*, the *Curlew*, and the *quaile ;*
These, and thy choicest viands do extend
    Their taste unto the lower end
Of thy glad table : not a dish more known
    To thee, then unto any one :   [*than*
But as thy meate, so thy *immortall Wine*
    Makes the smirk face of each to shine,
And spring fresh *Rose-buds*, while the salt, the wit
    Flowes from the Wine, and graces it :
While Reverence, waiting at the bashfull board,
    Honours my Lady and my Lord.
No scurrile jest; no open Sceane is laid
    Here, for to make the face affraid ;

---

[7] There seems to be no ancient authority for this name.
[8] = ? pewit or plover.   [9] = female of the 'ruffe.'
[1] 'Ruffes' are specially so called because they have a 'ruff' of feathers round their necks. Women used to wear articles round their necks called 'ruffs.'   [2] = a wild bird = corn-craik.

But temp'rate mirth dealt forth, and so discreet-
    ly that it makes the meate more sweet;
And adds perfumes unto the Wine, which thou
    Do'st rather poure forth, then allow   [*than*
By cruse and measure; thus devoting Wine,
    As the *Canary* Isles were thine :[3]
But with that wisdome, and that method, as
    No One that's there his guilty glasse
Drinks of distemper, or ha's cause to cry
    Repentance to his liberty.
No, thou know'st order, Ethicks, and ha's read
    All Oeconomicks, know'st to lead
A House-dance neatly, and can'st truly show,
    How farre a Figure ought to go,
Forward, or backward, side-ward, and what pace
    Can give, and what retract[4] a grace;
What Gesture, Courtship; Comliness agrees,
    With those thy primitive decrees,
To give subsistance to thy house, and proofe,
    What *Genii* support thy roofe,
Goodnes and *Greatnes;* not the oaken Piles;
    For these, and marbles have their whiles
To last, but not their ever : Vertues Hand
    It is, which builds, 'gainst Fate to stand.

[3] From whence came the wine so named.   [4] = retrace.

Such is thy house, whose firme foundations trust
　　　　Is more in thee, then in her dust,　　　　[*than*
Or depth ; these last may yeeld, and yearly shrinke,
　　　　When what is strongly built, no chinke
Or yawning rupture can the same devoure,
　　　　But fixt it stands, by her own power,
And well-laid bottome, on the iron and rock,
　　　　Which tryes, and counter-stands the shock,
And *Ramme* of time, and by vexation growes
　　　　The stronger : *Vertue dies when foes*
Are wanting to her exercise,[5] *but great*
　　　　And large she spreads by dust, and sweat.
Safe stand thy Walls, and Thee, and so both will,
　　　　Since neithers height was rais'd by th'ill
Of others ; since no Stud, no Stone, no Piece,
　　　　Was rear'd up by the Poore-mans fleece :
No Widowes Tenement was rackt to guild
　　　　Or fret thy Seeling, or to build　　　　[*ceiling*
A *Sweating-Closset*, to annoint the silke-
　　　　soft-skin, or bath in *Asses milke :*
No *Orphans* pittance, left him, serv'd to set
　　　　The pillars up of *lasting Jet,*

---

[5] So Montaigne.　He who does well is not necessarily virtuous.
" For it seemeth that the verie name of vertue presupposeth difficul-
tie and inferreth resistance, and cannot well exercise it selfe without
an enemie."—Florio's Montaigne (1613) p. 233.

For which their cryes might beate against thine eares,
    Or in the dampe Jet read their Teares.
No *Planke* from *Hallowed* Altar, do's appeale
    To yond' *Star-chamber*,[6] or do's seale
A curse to Thee, or Thine ; but all things even
    Make for thy peace, and pace to heaven.
Go on directly so, as just men may
    A thousand times, more sweare, then say, [*than*
This is that *Princely Pemberton*, who can
    Teach man to keepe a God in man :
And when wise Poets shall search out to see
    Good men, *They find them all in Thee.*

To his Valentine, *on* S. Valentines *day.*

OFT have I heard both Youths and Virgins say,
    Birds chuse their Mates, and couple too, this
        day :
But by their flight I never can divine,
When I shall couple with my Valentine.

Upon Doll. *Epig.*

DOLL she so soone began the wanton trade ;
    She ne'r remembers that she was a maide.

[6] Cf. Herbert : also Spelman on Sacrilege.

Upon Skrew. *Epig.*

S*KREW* lives by shifts ; yet sweares by no small
    oathes ;
For all his shifts, he cannot shift his clothes.

Upon Linnit. *Epig.*

L*INNIT* playes rarely on the Lute, we know ;
    And sweetly sings, but yet his breath sayes no.

Upon M. Ben. Johnson.[7] *Epig.*

A FTER the rare Arch-Poet JOHNSON dy'd,
    The Sock grew loathsome, and the Buskins pride,
Together with the Stages glory stood
Each like a poore and pitied widowhood.
The Cirque prophan'd was ; and all postures rackt :
For men did strut, and stride, and stare, not act.
Then temper[8] flew from words ; and men did squeake,
Looke red, and blow, and bluster, but not speake :
No Holy-Rage, or frantick-fires did stirre,
Or flash about the spacious Theater.
No clap of hands, or shout, or praises-proofe
Did crack the Play-house sides, or cleave her roofe.

---

[7] See Memorial-Introduction.
[8] In sense of moderation, as in the verbs temper and attemper.

Artlesse[9] *the Sceane was*; and that monstrous sin
Of deep and *arrant ignorance* came in ;
Such ignorance as theirs was, who once hist
At thy unequal'd Play, the *Alchymist :*[1]
Oh fie upon 'em ! Lastly too, all witt
In utter darkenes did, and still will sit
Sleeping the lucklesse Age out, till that she
Her Resurrection ha's again with Thee.

Another.

THOU had'st the wreath before, now take the
      Tree ;
That henceforth none be *Laurel-crown'd but Thee.*

To his Nephew, to be prosperous in his art af Painting.[2]

ON, as thou hast begunne, brave youth, and get
      The Palme from *Urbin*,[3] *Titian,* Tintarret,[4]
Brugel[5] and *Coxu*,[6] and the workes out-doe,
Of *Holben*,[7] and That mighty Ruben[8] too.
So draw, and paint, as none may do the like,
No, not the glory of the World, *Vandike.*[9]

---

[9] = without art.   [1] First played in 1610.
[2] See Memorial-Introduction.   [3] Raphael.   [4] Tintoretto.
[5] Breugel.   [6] Michael Coxcie, the Flemish painter.
[7] Holbein.   [8] Rubens.   [9] Vandyke.

Upon Glasse.   *Epig.*

GLASSE, out of deepe, and out of desp'rate want,
    Turn'd, from a Papist here, a Predicant.[1]
A Vicarige at last *Tom Glasse* got here,
Just upon five and thirty pounds a yeare.
Adde to that thirty five, but five pounds more,
He'l turn a Papist, rancker then before.   [*than*

A Vow to Mars.

STORE of courage to me grant,
    Now I'm turn'd a combatant :
Helpe me so, that I my *shield*,
(Fighting) lose not in the field.
That's the greatest shame of all,
That in warfare can befall.
Do but this ; and there shall be
Offer'd up a Wolfe to thee.

To his Maid Prew.

THESE *Summer-Birds*[2] did with thy master stay
    The times of warmth ; but then they flew away ;
Leaving their Poet (being now grown old)
Expos'd to all the comming Winters cold.

---

[1] = preacher.   [2] Cf. Herbert's " Summer friends."

But thou, *kind Prew*, did'st with my fates abide,
As well the Winters, as the Summers Tide :
For which thy love, live with thy master here,
Not one, but all the seasons of the yeare.

A Canticle to Apollo.

1. PLAY, *Phœbus* on thy Lute ;
   And we will sit all mute :
   By listning to thy Lire,
   That sets all eares on fire.

2. Hark, harke, the God do's play !
   And as he leads the way
   Through heaven, the very Speres,   [*spheres*
   As men, turne all to eares.

A just man.

A JUST man's like a Rock that turnes the wroth
   Of all the raging Waves, into a froth.[3]

Upon a hoarse Singer.

SING me to death ; for till thy voice be cleare,
   'Twill never please the pallate of mine eare.

---

[3] See Glossarial Index s. v.   Horace : Justum ac tenacem : Od.
iii. 3. 1.

How Pansies *or* Hart-ease *came first.*

FROLLICK Virgins once these were,
    Over-loving, (living here :)
Being here their ends deny'd
Ranne for Sweet-hearts mad, and di'd.
Love in pitie of their teares,
And their losse in blooming yeares ;
For their restlesse here-spent houres,
Gave them *Hearts-ease* turn'd to flow'rs.

To his peculiar friend Sir Edward Fish, *Knight Baronet.*[4]

SINCE for thy full deserts (with all the rest
    Of these chaste spirits, that are here possest
Of Life eternall) Time has made thee one,
For growth in this my rich Plantation :
Live here : But know 'twas vertue, & not chance,
That gave thee this so high inheritance.
Keepe it forever ; grounded with the good,
Who hold fast here an endlesse lively-hood.

---

[4] There is no record of his creation as a baronet, but he was evidently recognized as one, as letters of administration to his estate as Sir Edward Fish, Bart., of Chertsey co. Surrey, were granted 10th Nov., 1658, to his only son, Sir Edward Fish, Bart.

Larr's *portion, and the* Poets *part.*

AT my homely Country-seat,
    I have there a little wheat ;
Which I worke to Meale, and make
Therewithall a *Holy-cake :*
Part of which I give to *Larr*,[5]
Part is my peculiar.

Upon man.

MAN is compos'd here of a two-fold part ;
    The first of Nature, and the next of Art :
Art presupposes Nature ; Nature shee
Prepares the way for mans docility.

Liberty.

THOSE ills that mortall men endure
    So long are capable of cure,
As they of freedome may be sure :
But that deni'd ; a griefe, though small,
Shakes the whole Roofe, or ruines all.

Lots to be liked.

LEARN this of me, where e'r thy Lot doth fall ;
    Short lot, or not, to be content with all.

---

[5] See Glossarial Index s. v. There is a primary allusion to what was offered to the Lar or Lares.

Griefes.

J*OVE* may afford us thousands of reliefs ;
Since man expos'd is to a world of griefs.

Upon Eeles. *Epig.*

E*ELES* winds and turnes, and cheats and steales
yet *Eeles*
Driving these sharking trades, is out at heels.

The Dreame.

B Y Dream I saw, one of the three
Sisters of Fate, appeare to me.
Close to my Beds side she did stand
Shewing me there a fire brand ;
She told me too, as that did spend,
So drew my life unto an end.
Three quarters were consum'd of it ;
Onely remaind a little bit,
Which will be burnt up by and by,
Then *Julia* weep, for I must dy.

Upon Raspe. *Epig.*

R *ASPE* playes at Nine-holes; and 'tis known he
gets
Many a Teaster [6] by his game, and bets :

[6] *i. e.* tester : $= 6d.$

But of his gettings there's but little sign ;
When one hole wasts more then he gets by Nine. [*than*

Upon Center *a Spectacle-maker with a*
flat nose.

CENTER is known weak sighted, and he sells
    To others store of helpfull spectacles.
Why weres [7] he none ?   Because we may suppose,
Where *Leaven* wants, there *Levill* lies the nose.

Clothes do but cheat and
cousen us.

AWAY with silks, away with Lawn,
    Ile have no Sceans, or Curtains drawn :
Give me my Mistresse, as she is,
Drest in her nak't simplicities :
For as my Heart, ene so mine Eye
Is wone with flesh, not *Drapery*.

To Dianeme.

SHEW me thy feet ; shew me thy legs, thy thighes ;
    Shew me Those *Fleshie Principalities ;*

___

[7] = wears.

Shew me that Hill (where smiling Love doth sit)
Having a living Fountain under it.
Shew me thy waste ;[8] then let me there withall,
By the *Assention* [9] of thy Lawn, see All. *linen*

Upon Electra.

WHEN out of bed my Love doth spring,
    'Tis but as day a-kindling :
But when She's up and fully drest,
'Tis then *broad Day throughout the East.*

To his Booke.

HAVE I not blest Thee ?   Then go forth ; nor
      fear
Or spice, or fish, or fire, or close-stools here.
But with thy fair Fates leading thee, Go on
With thy most white *Predestination.*[1]
Nor thinke these Ages that do hoarcely sing
The *farting Tanner*, and *familiar King ;*
The *dancing Frier*, tatter'd in the bush ;
Those monstrous lies of little *Robin Rush :*
Tom Chipperfeild, and pritty-*lisping Ned*,
That doted on a Maide of *Gingerbred :*

---

[8] See Glossarial Index s. v.   [9] = ascension.
[1] See Glossarial Index s. v.

The *flying Pilcher*, and the *frisking Dace*,
With all the rabble of *Tim-Trundells* race,
(Bred from the dung-hils, and adulterous rhimes,[2])
Shall live, and thou not superlast [3] all times?
No, no, thy Stars have destin'd Thee to see
The whole world die, and turn to dust with thee.
He's greedie of his life, who will not fall,
Whenas a publick ruine bears down All.

Of Love.

I DO not love, nor can it be
    Love will in vain spend shafts on me :
I did this God-head once defie ;
Since which I freeze, but cannot frie.[4]
Yet out, alas ! the deaths the same,
Kil'd by a frost or by a flame.

Upon himself.

I DISLIKT but even now ;
    Now I love I know not how.

[2] Of the street ballads and chap books, e. g., " The Historie of Friar Rush, how he came to a House of Religion to seek a Service, and being entertained by the Prior was made First Cook, being full of pleasant Mirth and Delight for young people." See Memorial-Intoduction for more on these allusions.   [3] = out-last.

[4] See Glossarial Index s. v.

Was I idle, and that while
Was I fier'd with a smile ?
Ile too [5] work, or pray; and then
I shall quite dislike agen.

Another.

LOVE he that will ; it best likes me,
  To have my neck from Loves yoke free.

Upon Skinns. *Epig.*

KINNS he dined well to day ; how do you think ?
  His Nails they were his meat, his Reume the
    drink.

Upon Pievish. *Epig.*

PIEVISH doth boast, that he's the very first
  Of English Poets, and 'tis thought the Worst.

Upon Jolly *and* Jilly.
Epig.

JOLLY and *Jillie*, bite and scratch all day,
  But yet get children (as the neighbours say.)
The reason is, though all the day they fight,
They cling and close, some minutes of the night.

[5] = to.

The mad Maids song.[6]

1. GOOD morrow to the Day so fair ;
   Good morning Sir to you :
   Good morrow to mine own torn hair
   Bedabled [7] with the dew.

2. Good morning to this Prim-rose too ;
   Good morrow to each maid ;
   That will with flowers the *Tomb* bestrew,
   Wherein my Love is laid.

3. Ah ! woe is mee, woe, woe is me,
   Alack and welladay !
   For pitty, Sir, find out that Bee,
   Which bore my Love away.

4. I'le seek him in your *Bonnet* brave ;[8]
   Ile seek him in your eyes ;
   Nay, now I think th'ave made his grave
   I'th'bed of strawburies.

5. Ile seek him there ; I know, ere this,
   The cold, cold Earth doth shake him ;

---

[6] See Memorial-Introduction on this supremest of Herrick's Lyrics.
[7] = bedewed : see Glossarial Index s. v.
[8] Query—allusion to the phrase for madness, 'a bee in the bonnet'?

But I will go, or send a kisse
   By you, Sir, to awake him.

6. Pray hurt him not; though he be dead,
   He knowes well who do love him,
And who with green-turfes reare his head,
   And who do rudely move him.

7. He's soft and tender (Pray take heed)
   With bands of Cow-slips bind him;
And bring him home; but 'tis decreed,
   That I shall never find him.

To Springs and Fountains.

I HEARD ye co'd coole heat; and came
   With hope you would allay the same:
Thrice I have washt, but feel no cold,
Nor find that true, which was foretold.
Methinks like mine, your pulses beat;
And labour with unequall heat:
Cure, cure your selves, for I discrie,
Ye boil with Love, as well as I.

Upon Julia's *unlacing*
her self.

TELL, if thou canst (and truly) whence doth come
   This *Camphire, Storax,*[9] *Spiknard, Galbanum:*

[9] = Syrian gum.

These *Musks*, these *Ambers*, and those other smells
(Sweet as the *Vestrie*[1] of the *Oracles*.)
Ile tell thee ; while my *Julia* did unlace
Her silken bodies,[2] but a breathing space :
The passive Aire such odour then assum'd,
As when to *Jove* Great *Juno* goes perfum'd.[3]
Whose pure-Immortall body doth transmit
A scent, that fills both Heaven and Earth with it.

To Bacchus, *a Canticle*.[4]

WHITHER dost thou whorry [5] me,
    Bacchus, being full of thee ?
This way, that way, that way, this,
Here, and there a fresh Love is.
That doth like me, this doth please ;
Thus a thousand Mistresses,
I have now ; yet I alone,
  · Having All, injoy not *One*.

[1] = vestures ? or rooms ?   [2] = bodice.
[3] This is another of Herrick's mentionings of Juno's odour. Whence did he get the idea ? It is not in Homer's famous account of her embracing Jupiter.
[4] Ll. 1-2 imitation of Horace, Quo me, Bacche, &c. (Od. iii. 25, 1-2.)   [5] = hurry : it also means to 'teaze' and 'fidget.'

The Lawne.

WO'D I see Lawn, clear as the Heaven, and thin ?
  It sho'd be onely in my *Julia's* skin :
Which so betrayes her blood, as we discover
The blush of cherries, when a Lawn's cast over.

The Frankincense.

WHEN my off'ring next I make,
    Be thy hand the hallowed Cake :
And thy brest the Altar, whence
Love may smell the *Frankincense.*

Upon Patrick *a footman.   Epig.*

NOW *Patrick* [6] with his footmanship has done,
    His eyes and ears strive which sho'd fastest run.

Upon Bridget.   *Epig.*

OF foure teeth onely *Bridget* was possest ;
    Two she spat out, a cough forc't out the rest. [7]

To Sycamores.

I'm sick of Love ; [8] O let me lie
    Under your shades, to sleep or die !

---

[6] The running footmen were generally Irish.
[7] Martial.   [8] = sick-of-love, a quibble on Sycamores.

Either is welcome ; so I have
Or here my Bed, or here my Grave.
Why do you sigh, and sob, and keep
Time with the tears, that I do weep?
Say, have ye sence, or do you prove
What *Crucifixions* are in Love ?
I know ye do ; and that's the why,
You sigh for Love, as well as I.

A Pastorall sung to the King :
Montano, Silvio, *and* Mirtillo, *Shepheards.*

Mon. BAD are the times.   *Sil.* And wors then
         they are we.   [*than*
Mon. Troth, bad are both ; worse fruit, and ill the
        tree :
The feast of Shepheards fail.[9]   *Sil.* None crowns the
        cup
Of *Wassaile* now, or sets the *quintell*[1] up :
And He, who us'd to leade the Country-round,
Youthfull *Mirtillo*, Here he comes, Grief-drownd.
  Ambo. Lets cheer him up.   *Sil.* Behold him weep-
      ing ripe.
  Mirt. Ah ! *Amarillis*, farewell mirth and pipe ;

---

[9] Agrees with nearest noun, as in Shakespeare.   [1] =quintain.

Since thou art gone, no more I mean to play,

To these smooth Lawns, my mirthfull Roundelay.[2]

Dear *Amarillis!*   *Mon.* Hark!   *Sil.* mark: *Mir.*
    this earth grew sweet

Where, *Amarillis*, Thou didst set thy feet.[3]

    Ambo. Poor pittied youth!   *Mir.* And here the
    breth of kine

And sheep, grew more sweet, by that breth of Thine.

This flock [4] of wooll, and this rich lock of hair,

This ball of *Cow-slips*, these she gave me here.

    Sil. Words sweet as Love it self.   *Montano*, Hark.

    Mirt. This way she came, and this way too she went;

How each thing smells divinely redolent!

Like to a field of beans,[5] when newly blown;

Or like a medow being lately mown.

    Mont. A sweet-sad passion.——

    Mirt. In dewie-mornings when she came this way,

Sweet Bents [6] wode bow, to give my Love the day:

---

[2] = here, the music of a ' dance.'   Cf. ' pipe' and ' play ': dance music that begins and ends with the same strain.

[3] See Glossarial Index s. v.

[4] = lock of wool.

[5] See Glossarial Index: and Sidney:—" O breath more sweet than is the blooming bean."

[6] = rushes or grass.   " The flower she touch'd on, dipp'd and rose and turn'd to look at her," Tennyson, Talking Oak.

And when at night, she folded had her sheep,
Daysies wo'd shut, and closing, sigh and weep.
Besides (Ai me !) since she went hence to dwell,
The voices Daughter [7] nea'r spake syllable.
But she is gone. *Sil. Mirtillo*, tell us whether:
   Mirt. Where she and I shall never meet together.
   Mont. Fore-fend [8] it *Pan*, and *Palès* do thou please
To give an end : *Mir.* To what ? *Sil.* such griefs
      as these.
   Mirt. Never, O never ! Still I may endure
The wound I suffer, never find a cure.
   Mont. Love for thy sake will bring her to these hills
And dales again : *Mir.* No, I will languish still ;
And all the while my part shall be to weepe ;
And with my sighs, call home my bleating sheep :
And in the Rind of every comely tree
Ile carve thy name,[9] and in that name kisse thee :
   Mont. Set with the Sunne, thy woes : *Sil.* The
      day grows old :
And time it is our full-fed flocks to fold.
   Chor. The shades grow great; but greater growes
      our sorrow,

---

[7] = Echo.   [8] = forbid.   [9] See again the " Talking
Oak." See also Memorial-Introduction for parallel from Stanley.

But lets go steepe
Our eyes in sleepe;
And meet to weepe
    To morrow.

The Poet loves a Mistresse, but not
to marry.

1. I DO not love to wed,
    Though I do like to wooe;
    And for a maidenhead
    Ile beg, and buy it too.

2. Ile praise, and Ile approve
    Those maids that never vary;
    And fervently Ile love;
    But yet I would not marry.

3. Ile hug, Ile kisse, Ile play,
    And Cock-like, Hens Ile tread:
    And sport it any way;
    But in the Bridall Bed:

4. For why? that man is poore,
    Who hath but one of many;
    But crown'd he is with store,
    That single may have any.

Why then, say, what is he
(To freedome so unknown)
Who having two or three,
Will be content with one ?

Upon Flimsey. *Epig.*

WHY walkes *Nick Flimsey* like a Male-content ?
    Is it because his money all is spent ?
No, but because the Ding-thrift [1] now is poore,
And knowes not where i'th world to borrow more.

Upon Shewbread. *Epig.*

LAST night thou didst invite me home to eate ;
    And shew'st me there much Plate, but little
        meate.
Prithee, when next thou do'st invite, barre State,
And give me meate, or give me else thy Plate.

The Willow Garland.

A WILLOW Garland thou did'st send
    Perfum'd (last day) to me :
Which did but only this portend,
    I was forsooke by thee.

[1] spend-thrift.

Since so it is ; Ile tell thee what,
　　To morrow thou shalt see
Me weare the Willow ; after that,
　　To dye upon the Tree.

As Beasts unto the Altars go
　　With Garlands drest, so I
Will, with my Willow-wreath also,
　　Come forth and sweetly dye.

A Hymne to Sir Clipseby Crew.[2]

'TWAS not Lov's Dart ;
　　Or any blow
Of want, or'foe,
Did wound my heart
With an eternall smart :

　　But only you,
　　My sometimes known
　　Companion,
　　(My dearest *Crew,*)
That me unkindly slew.

　　May your fault dye,
　　And have no name
　　In Bookes of fame ;

---

[2] Here is a little quarrel.　See Memorial-Introduction.

Or let it lye
Forgotten now, as I.

We parted are,
And now no more,
As heretofore,
By jocund Larr,[3]
Shall be familiar.

But though we Sever
My *Crew* shall see,
That I will be
Here faithlesse never ;
But love my *Clipseby* ever.

Upon Roots.   *Epig.*

ROOTS had no money ; yet he went o'th score
    For a wrought Purse ; can any tell wherefore ?
Say, What sho'd *Roots* do with a Purse in print,
That h'ad nor Gold nor Silver to put in't ?

Upon Craw.

CRAW cracks in sirrop ; and do's stinking say,
    Who can hold that (my friends) that will away ?

[3] See Glossarial Index s. v.

Observation.

WHO to the North, or South, doth set
   His Bed, Male children shall beget.

Empires.

EMPIRES of Kings, are now, and ever were,
   (As *Salust* saith)[4] co-incident to feare.

Felicity, quick of flight.

EVERY time seemes short to be,
   That's measur'd by felicity :
But one halfe houre, that's made up here
With griefe ; seemes longer then a yeare.   [*than*

Putrefaction.

PUTREFACTION is the end
   Of all that Nature doth entend.[5]

Passion.

WERE there not a Matter known,
   There wo'd be no Passion.

---

[4] Sallust : but where ?   [5] = purpose.

Jack *and* Jill.

SINCE *Jack* and *Jill* both wicked be ;
It seems a wonder unto me,
That they no better do agree.

Upon Parson Beanes.

OLD Parson *Beanes* hunts six dayes of the week,
And on the seaventh, he has his Notes to seek.
Six dayes he hollows so much breath away,
That on the seaventh, he can nor preach, or pray.

The crowd and company.

IN holy meetings, there a man may be
One of the crowd, not of the companie.[6]

Short and long both likes.

THIS Lady's short, that Mistresse she is tall ;
But long or short, I'm well content with all.

Pollicie in Princes.

THAT Princes may possèsse a surer seat,
'Tis fit they make no One with them too great.

---

[6] " A crowd is not company." Bacon's Essays.   Here ı the sly meaning is, not of the ' company ' [of saints].

Upon Rook. *Epig.*

ROOK he sells feathers,[7] yet he still doth crie
    Fie on this pride, this Female vanitie.
Thus, though the Rooke do's raile against the sin,
He loves the gain that vanity brings in.

Upon the Nipples of Julia's *Breast.*

HAVE ye beheld (with much delight)
    A red-Rose peeping through a white?
Or else a Cherrie (double grac't)
Within a Lillie-center [8] plac't?
Or ever mark't the pretty beam, –
A Strawberry shewes halfe drown'd in Creame?
Or seen rich Rubies blushing through
A pure smooth Pearle, and Orient too?
So like to this, nay all the rest,
Is each neate Niplet[9] of her breast.

To Daisies, *not to shut so soone.*

1. SHUT not so soon; the dull-ey'd night
    Ha's not as yet begunne

---

[7] It was an often-repeated sarcasm that the Puritans of Black-friars were (most inconsistently) feather-makers.

[8] Misprinted 'Within a Lillie? Center plac't?' Is it possible the '?' was meant for a long 'f' and so = 'Lillie's.'   [9] = tiny nipple.

To make a seisure on the light,
   Or to seale up the Sun.

2. No Marigolds yet closèd are;
      No shadowes great appeare;
   Nor doth the early Shepheards Starre
      Shine like a spangle here.

3. Stay but till my *Julia* close
      Her life-begetting eye;
   And let the whole world then dispose
      It selfe to live or dye.

To the little Spinners.[1]

YEE pretty Huswives, wo'd ye know
   The worke that I wo'd put ye to?
This, this it sho'd be, for to spin,
A Lawn for me, so fine and thin,
As it might serve me for my skin.
For cruell Love ha's me so whipt,
That of my skin, I all am stript;
And shall dispaire, that any art
Can ease the rawnesse, or the smart;
Unlesse you skin again each part.

[1] = Spiders.

Which mercy if you will but do,
I call all Maids to witnesse too
What here I promise, that no Broom
Shall now, or ever after come
To wrong a *Spinner* or her Loome.

Oberons *Palace.*

AFTER the Feast (my *Shapcot*) see,
    The Fairie Court I give to thee :
Where we'le present our *Oberon*, led
Halfe tipsie to the Fairie Bed,
Where *Mab* he finds ; who there doth lie
Not without mickle majesty.
Which, done ; and thence remov'd the light,
We'l wish both Them and Thee, good night.

Full as a Bee with Thyme, and Red,
As Cherry harvest, now high fed
For Lust and action ; on he'l go,
To lye with *Mab*, though all say no.
Lust ha's no eares ; He's sharpe as thorn ;
And fretfull, carries Hay in's horne,[2]

---

[2] = Fœnum habet in cornu. (Sat. i. 4. 34.) The meaning is = shows he's outrageous or dangerous. Cows that are wild and dangerous have still sometimes a tuft of hay round the tip of one horn to forewarn all comers. It is also the index of a bad-tempered cow, which goes bellowing about and sticking its horn (always one only) into the ground, and tearing up tufts of grass, &c., which, adhering, show plainly the temper of the beast.

And lightning in his eyes ; and flings
Among the Elves, (if mov'd) the stings
Of peltish[3] wasps ; well[4] know his Guard
Kings though th'are hated, will be fear'd.
Wine lead him on.   Thus to a Grove
(Sometimes [5] devoted unto Love)
Tinseld with *Twilight,* He, and They
Lead by the shine of Snails ; a way
Beat with their num'rous [6] feet, which by
Many a neat perplexity,
Many a turn, and man' a crosse-
Track they redeem[7] a bank of mosse
Spungie and swelling, and farre more
Soft then the finest Lemster[8] Ore.   [*than*
Mildly disparkling, like those fiers,
Which break from the Injeweld tyres
Of curious Brides ; or like those mites
Of Candi'd dew in Moony nights.
Upon this *Convex,* all the flowers,
(Nature begets by th' Sun, and showers,)

---

[3] = fretful, angry.   [4] Misprinted ' we'l.'
[5] = sometime.   [6] = metrical, rhythmic.
[7] Query—deck (Latin redimio) ? See " Upon this Convex," &c.
a few lines onward.   Or is it = regain ?
[8] = Leominster wool, often referred to on account of its whiteness
—with a sub-reference in ' ore ' to its being the staple : and hence
the riches (equal to ore) of the place and district.

Are to a wilde digestion brought,

As if Love's *Sampler* here was wrought :

Or *Citherea's Ceston*,[9] which

All with temptation doth bewitch.

Sweet Aires move here ; and more divine

Made by the breath of great ey'd-kine,

Who as they lowe, empearl with milk

The four-leav'd grasse, or mosse, like [10] silk.

The breath of *Munkies* met to mix

With *Musk-flies*, are th' *Aromaticks*.

Which cense this Arch ; and here and there,

And farther off, and every where,

Throughout that *Brave Mosaick* yard

Those Picks [11] or Diamonds in the Card :

With peeps of Harts, of Club and Spade,

Are here most neatly inter-laid.

Many a Counter,[1] many a Die,

Half rotten, and without an eye,

Lies here abouts ; and for to pave

The excellency of this Cave,

Squirrils and childrens teeth late shed,

Are neatly here enchequerèd.

---

[9] = cestus.   [10] Misprinted ' mosse-like.'

[11] = picks, i.e. diamonds : Grose, 'a spade' : the French *picque* is a spade.

[1] = counters such as are used in gambling, and dice with their pips (or eyes) worn off.

With brownest *Toadstones*,[2] and the Gum
That shines upon the blewer Plum.
The nails faln off by Whit-flawes :[3] Art's ·
Wise hand enchasing here those warts,
Which we to others (from our selves)
Sell, and brought hither by the Elves.
The tempting Mole, stoln from the neck
Of the shie Virgin, seems to deck
The holy Entrance ; where within
The roome is hung with the blew skin
Of shifted Snake : enfreez'd[4] throughout
With eyes of Peacocks Trains, & Trout-
flies curious wings ; and these among
Those silver-pence, that cut the tongue
Of the red infant, neatly hung.[5]
The glow-wormes eyes ; the shining scales
Of silv'rie fish ; wheat-strawes, the snailes
Soft Candle-light ;[6] the Kitling's eyne ;[7]
Corrupted wood ;[8] serve here for shine.
No glaring light of bold-fac't Day,
Or other over-radiant Ray

[2] = infants.   [3] See Glossarial Index s. v.
[4] = en-friezed, i. e. adorned as is a ' frieze.'
[5] Folk-lore = tongue-tied.
[6] Query—his shining track ? or is it phosphorous ?
[7] See Glossarial Index, s. v.   [8] = wood that is phosphorescent.

Ransacks this roome ; but what weak beams
Can make reflected from these jems,
And multiply ; Such is the light,
But ever doubtfull Day, or night.
By this quaint Taper-light he winds
His Errours⁹ up ; and now he finds
His Moon-tann'd *Mab*, as somewhat sick,
And (Love knowes) tender as a chick.
Upon six plump *Dandillions*, high-
Rear'd, lyes her Elvish-majestie :
Whose woollie-bubbles¹⁰ seem'd to drowne
Hir *Mab-ship* in obedient Downe.
For either sheet, was spread the Caule
That doth the Infants face enthrall,
When it is born : (by some enstyl'd.
The luckie *Omen* of the child)¹¹
And next to these two blankets ore-
Cast of the finest *Gossamore.*
And then a Rug of carded wooll,
Which, *Spunge-like* drinking in the dull-
Light of the Moon, seem'd to comply,¹²
Cloud-like, the *daintie Deitie.*

⁹ = Wanderings.   ¹⁰ = she is lying upon the wooly-spheres of
six dandelions gone to seed.   ¹¹ Still advertised for often in sea-
ports : = that he will not be drowned.
¹² = enfold.

Thus soft she lies : and over-head
A *Spinners* [1] circle is bespread,
With Cob-web-curtains : from the roof
So neatly sunck,[2] as that no proof
Of any tackling can declare
What gives it hanging in the Aire.
The Fringe about this, are those *Threds*
Broke at the Losse of *Maiden-heads :*
And all behung with these pure Pearls,
Dropt from the eyes of *ravisht Girles*
Or writhing Brides ; when (panting) they
Give unto Love the straiter way.
For Musick now ; He has the cries
Of fain d-lost-Virginities ;
The which the *Elves* make to excite
A more unconquer'd appetite.
The Kings undrest ; and now upon
The Gnats-watch-word the *Elves* are gone.
And now the bed, and *Mab* possest
Of this great-little-kingly-Guest ;
We'll nobly think, what's to be done,
He'll do no doubt ; *This flax is spun.* [3]

---

[1] = Spider   [2] = inserted.   [3] = this web is finished or this
matter is ended.

To his peculiar friend Master Thomas Shapcott, *Lawyer.*[4]

I'VE paid Thee, what I promis'd ; that's not All ;
　　Besides I give Thee here a Verse that shall
(When hence thy Circum-mortall-part is [5] gon)
Arch-like, hold up, *Thy Name's Inscription.*
Brave men can't die,[6] whose Candid [7] Actions are
Writ in the Poets Endlesse-Kalendar :
Whose *velome,*[8] and whose *volumne* is the Skie,
And the pure Starres the praising Poetrie.

　　　　　　　　　　　　　　　　Farewell.

To Julia *in the Temple.*

BESIDES us two, i' th' Temple here's not one
　　To make up now a Congregation.
Let's to the *Altar of perfumes* then go,
And say short Prayers ; and when we have done so,
Then we shall see, how in a little space,
Saints will come in to fill each Pew and Place.

---

[4] See Memorial-Introduction.
[5] See Glossarial Index under ' circum-'.
[6] Vixere fortes, &c. Horace (Od. iv. 9. 25-6 *etseqq.*)　　[7] = white.
[8] = vellum covering or binding.

To Oenone.

1. WHAT Conscience, say, is it in thee
       When I a Heart had one,
   To Take away that Heart from me,
       And to retain Thy own?

2. For shame or pitty now encline
       To play a loving part;
   Either to send me kindly thine,
       Or give me back my heart.

3. Covet not both; but if thou dost
       Resolve to part with neither;
   Why! yet to shew that thou art just,
       Take me and mine together.

His weaknesse in woes.

I CANNOT suffer; and in this, my part
Of Patience wants. *Grief breaks the stoutest
Heart.*

Fame makes us forward.

TO Print our Poems, the propulsive cause
   Is Fame, (the breath of popular applause.)

To Groves.

YEE silent shades, whose each tree here
    Some Relique of a Saint doth weare :
Who for some sweet-hearts sake, did prove
The fire, and martyrdome of love.
Here is the Legend of those Saints
That di'd for love ; and their complaints :
Their wounded hearts ; and names we find
Encarv'd upon the Leaves and Rind.
Give way, give way to me, who come
Scorch't with the selfe-same martyrdome :
And have deserv'd as much (Love knowes)
As to be canoniz'd 'mongst those,
Whose deeds, and deaths here written are
Within your *Greenie-Kalendar :*
By all those Virgins Fillets hung
Upon your Boughs, and Requiems sung
For Saints and Soules departed hence,
(Here honour'd still with Frankincense)
By all those teares that have been shed,
As a *Drink-offering,* to the dead :
By all those True-love-knots, that be
With Motto's carv'd on every tree,
By sweet S. *Phillis ;*[9] pitie me :

[9] This is merely Phillis (the usual sweetheart maid) sainted.

By deare S. *Iphis ;*[10] and the rest,
Of all those other Saints now blest ;
Me, me, forsaken, here admit
Among your Mirtles to be writ :
That my poore name may have the glory
To live remembred in your story.

An Epitaph upon a Virgin.

HERE a solemne Fast we keepe,
    While all beauty lyes asleep
Husht be all things ; (no noyse here)
But the toning of a teare :
Or a sigh of such as bring
Cowslips for her covering.

To the right gratious Prince, Lodwick, Duke of Richmond and Lenox.[11]

OF all those three-brave-brothers, faln i' th'
    Warre,
(Not without glory) Noble Sir, you are,

---

[10] This is the mythological boy (the representative of the other sex) who hanged himself for love.

[11] Ludovic Stuart, 2d Duke of Lennox : born 29th Sep., 1574 : succeeded to the title on the death of his father, Esme, 28th May, 1583 : created Duke of Richmond 17th May, 1623 : married 1st Lady

Despite of all concussions left the Stem
To shoot forth Generations like to them.
Which may be done, if (Sir) you can beget
Men in their substance, not in counterfeit.
Such Essences as those Three Brothers ; known
Eternall by their own production.
Of whom, from Fam's white [1] Trumpet, This Ile Tell,·
Worthy their everlasting Chronicle :
Never since first *Bellona* us'd a Shield,
Such Three brave Brothers fell in Mars *his Field.*
These were those Three *Horatii Rome* did boast,
Rom's [2] were these *Three Horatii* we have lost.   ·
One *Cordelion* had that Age long since ;
This, Three ; which Three, you make up Foure
      Brave Prince.

To Jealousie.

1. O JEALOUSIE, that art
         The Canker of the heart :

Sophia Ruthven, d. of William, 1st Earl of Gowrie : 2dly, Jean, d.
of Sir Matthew Campbell, of London, Kt. : 3dly, Lady Frances
Howard, only d. of Thomas, 1st Viscount Brindon.   He died 16th
Feb., 1623-4, and was buried the next day in Westminster Abbey.
This is another of Herrick's youthful poems.   See Memorial-Intro-
duction for further details.

   [1] See Glossarial Index s. v.
   [2] =Romans : I correct misprint of ' where ' for ' were ' here.

And mak'st all hell
Where thou do'st dwell;
For pitie be
No *Furie*, or no *Fire-brand* to me.

2. Farre from me Ile remove
All thoughts of irksome Love:
And turn to snow,
Or Christall grow;
To keep still free
(O ! Soul-tormenting Jealousie,) from Thee.

To live Freely.

LET'S live in hast; use pleasures while we may:
Co'd life return, 'twod never lose a day.

Upon Spunge. *Epig.*

SPUNGE makes his boasts that he's the onely man
Can hold of Beere and Ale an Ocean;
Is this his Glory? then his Triumph's Poore;
I know the *Tunne* of *Hidleberge* [3] holds more.

---

[3] Heidelberg : celebrated by Coryat and Davies of Hereford, is still one of the sights of the quaint old town.

His Almes.

H ERE, here I live,
　And somewhat give,
Of what I have,
To those, who crave.
Little or much,
My Almnes is such :
But if my deal
Of Oyl and Meal
Shall fuller grow,
More Ile bestow :
Mean time be it
E'en but a bit,
Or else a crum,
The scrip [4] hath some.

Upon himself.

C OME, leave this loathèd Country-life, and then
　Grow up to be a Roman *Citizen.*
Those mites of Time, which yet remain unspent,.
Waste thou in that most Civill Government.
Get their comportment, and the gliding tongue
Of those mild Men, thou art to live among :

[4] = wallet of the wayfarer or poor man.

Then being seated in that smoother *Sphere*,
Decree thy everlasting *Topick* [5] there.
And to the Farm-house nere return at all,
Though Granges [6] do not love thee, Cities shall.

To enjoy the Time.

WHILE Fates permit us, let's be merry ;
   Passe all we must the fatall Ferry :
And this our life too whirles away,
With the Rotation of the Day.

Upon Love.

1.   LOVE, I have broke
     Thy yoke ;
  The neck is free :
  But when I'm next
     Love-vext,
  Then shackell me.

2.   'Tis better yet
     To fret
  The feet or hands ;
  Then to enthrall,   [*than*
     Or gall
  The neck with bands.

[5] = abode : from the Greek original τόπος.   [6] = farm-houses.

To the Right Honourable Mildmay, *Earle*
    '*of* Westmorland.[7]

YOU are a Lord, an Earle, nay more, a Man,[8]
    Who writes sweet Numbers well as any can :
If so, why then are not These Verses hurld,
Like *Sybels* Leaves, throughout the ample world ?
What is a Jewell if it be not set
Forth by a ring, or some rich Carkanet ? [9]
But being so ; then the beholders cry,
See, see a Jemme (as rare as Bælus eye.[1])
Then publick praise do's runne upon the Stone,
For a most rich, a rare, a precious One.
Expose your jewels then unto the view,
That we may praise Them, or themselves prize You.
Vertue conceal'd (with Horace you'l confesse,)
Differs not much from drowzie slothfullnesse.[2]

---

[7] See former poem.   His volume of Poems called " Otia Sacra,"
&c., 1648, contains fine things.   See Memorial-Introduction.

[8] " He was a goodly king, he was a man :—take him," &c.
Hamlet, i. 2.   [9] See Glossarial Index s. v.

[1] = an Eastern gem so called by Pliny, and dedicated by the
Assryians to Belus.   [2] Horace : Ode iv. 9.

The Plunder.

I AM of all bereft ;
   Save but some few Beanes left,
Whereof (at last) to make,
For me, and mine a Cake :
Which eaten, they and I
Will say our grace, and die.

Littlenesse no cause of Leannesse.

ONE feeds on Lard, and yet is leane ;
   And I but feasting with a Beane,
Grow fat and smooth : The reason is,
Jove prospers my meat, more then his.   [*than*

Upon one who said she was alwayes young.

YOU say y'are young ; but when your Teeth are
   told
To be but three, Black-ey'd, wee'l thinke y'are old.

Upon Huncks. Epig.

HUNCKS ha's no money (he do's sweare, or say)
   About him, when the Taverns shot 's [3] to pay.
If he ha's none in 's pockets, trust me, *Huncks*
Ha's none at home, in Coffers, Desks, or Trunks.

[3] See Glossarial Index s. v.

The Jimmall[4] Ring, or True-love-knot.

THOU sent'st to me a True-love-knot ; but I
　　Return'd a Ring of Jimmals, to imply
Thy Love had one knot, mine a triple tye.

The parting Verse, or Charge to his supposed Wife when he travelled.[5]

GO hence, and with this parting kisse,
　　Which joyns two souls, remember this ;
Though thou beest young, kind, soft, and faire,
And may'st draw thousands with a haire :
Yet let these glib temptations be
Furies to others, Friends to me.
Looke upon all ; and though on fire
Thou set'st their hearts, let chaste desire
Steere Thee to me ; and thinke (me gone)
In having all, that thou hast none.
Nor so immurèd wo'd I have
Thee live, as dead and in thy grave ;
But walke abroad, yet wisely well
Stand for my comming, Sentinell.

[4] An example of how the gemmal, literally double or twin ring, was used for any linked ring, for here there were three, or possibly four hoops.

[5] See Memorial-Introduction on the Haslewood-Kingsborough MS. of this poem.

And think (as thou do'st walke the street)
Me, or my shadow thou do'st meet.
I know a thousand greedy eyes
Will on thy Feature tirannize,
In my short absence ; yet behold
Them like some Picture, or some Mould
Fashion'd like Thee ; which though 'tave eares
And eyes, it neither sees or heares.
Gifts will be sent, and Letters, which
Are the expressions of that itch,
And salt, which frets thy Suters ; fly
Both, lest thou lose thy liberty :
For that once lost, thou't fall to one,
Then prostrate to a million.
But if they wooe thee, do thou say,
(As that chaste Queen of *Ithaca*
Did to her suitors) this web done
(Undone as oft as done) I'm wonne ;
I will not urge Thee, for I know,
Though thou art young, thou canst say no,
And no again, and so deny,
Those thy Lust-burning *Incubi*.
Let them enstile [5] Thee Fairest faire,
The Pearle of Princes, yet despaire

[5] = entitle.

That so thou art, because thou must
Believe, Love speaks it not, but Lust;
And this their Flatt'rie do's commend
Thee chiefly for their pleasures end.
I am not jealous of thy Faith,
Or will be; for the Axiome saith,
He that doth still [6] suspect, do's haste
A gentle mind to be unchaste.
No, live thee to thy selfe, and keep
Thy thoughts as cold, as is thy sleep :
And let thy dreames be only fed
With this, that I am in thy bed.
And thou then turning in that Sphere,
Waking shalt find me sleeping there.
But yet if boundlesse Lust must skaile
Thy Fortress, and will needs prevaile ;
And wildly force a passage in,
Banish consent, and 'tis no sinne
Of Thine ; so *Lucrece* fell, and the
Chaste *Syracusian Cyane.*
So *Medullina* fell, yet none
Of these had imputation
For the least trespasse; 'cause the mind
Here was not with the act combin'd.

[6] I fill in ' still.'

The body sins not, 'tis the Will
That makes the Action, good, or ill.
And if thy fall sho'd this way come,
Triumph in such a Martirdome.
I will not over-long enlarge
To thee, this my religious charge.
Take this compression, so by this
Means, I shall know what other kisse
Is mixt with mine; and truly know,
Returning, if 't be mine or no:
Keepe it till then; and now my Spouse,
For my wisht safety pay thy vowes,
And prayers to *Venus*; if it please
The *great-blew-ruler* of the seas;[7]
Not many full-fac't-moons shall waine,
Lean-horn'd, before I come again
As one triumphant; when I find
In thee, all faith of Woman-kind.
Nor wo'd I have thee thinke, that Thou
Had'st power thy selfe to keep this vow;
But having scapt temptations shelfe,[8]
Know vertue taught thee, not thy selfe.

[7] Cf. Lovelace 'To Lucasta': "The foaming blue-god's rage."
[8] = reef.

To his Kinsman, Sir Tho. Soame.[9]

SEEING thee *Soame,* I see a Goodly man,
   And in that Good, a great *Patrician.*
Next to which Two ; among the City-Powers,
And Thrones, thy selfe one of Those Senatours
Not wearing Purple only for the show ;
(As many Conscripts of the Citie do)
But for True Service, worthy of that Gowne,
The *Golden* chain too, and the *Civick* Crown.

To Blossoms.

1. FAIRE pledges of a fruitfull Tree,
     Why do yee fall so fast ?
     Your date is not so past ;
  But you may stay yet here a while,
     To blush and gently smile ;
     And go at last.

2. What, were yee borne to be
     An houre or half's delight ;
     And so to bid goodnight ?
 'Twas pitie Nature brought yee forth
     Meerly to shew your worth,
     And lose you quite.

[9] See former note on Soame.

3. But you are lovely Leaves, where we
     May read how soon things have
     Their end, though ne'r so brave :
And after they have shown their pride,
     Like you a while : They glide
     Into the Grave.

Mans dying-place uncertain.

MAN knowes where first he ships himselfe ;
     but he
Never can tell, where shall his Landing be.

Nothing Free-cost.

NOTHING comes Free-cost here ; *Jove* will not
     let
His gifts go from him ; if not bought with sweat.

Few fortunate.

MANY we are, and yet but few possesse
     Those Fields of everlasting happinesse.

To Perenna.

HOW long, *Perenna*, wilt thou see
     Me languish for the love of Thee ?
Consent and play a friendly part
To save ; when thou may'st kill a heart.

To the Ladyes.

TRUST me Ladies, I will do
  Nothing to distemper you ;
If I any fret or vex,
Men they shall be, *not your sex.*

The Old Wives Prayer.

HOLY-ROOD come forth and shield
  Us i'th' Citie, and the Field :
Safely guard us, now and aye,
From the blast that burns by day ;
And those sounds that us affright
In the dead of dampish night. [1]
Drive all hurtfull Feinds us fro,
By the Time the Cocks first crow.

Upon a cheap Laundresse. Epig.

FEACIE (some say) doth wash her clothes i'th' Lie [1]
  That sharply trickles from her either eye.
The *Laundresses,* They envie her good-luck,
Who can with so small charges *drive the buck.* [2]

---

[1] = the alkaline solution (soda or potash, or ashes containing them) used in washing, &c.

[2] This is probably imitated from a similar bit in Ben Jonson's Tale of a Tub (Act iii. close). Buck refers to the clothes to be

What needs she fire and ashes to consume,
Who can scoure Linnens with her own salt *reeume?*

Upon his departure hence.

T HUS I
   Passe by,
And die :
As One,
Unknown,
And gon :
I'm made
A shade,
And laid
I'th grave :
There have
My Cave.
Where tell
I dwell,
Farewell.

---

washed, but in what way is not .known. To 'drive a buck' is to
wash the buck; but the exact meaning is also unknown. The
phrase may be derived from beating the clothes with the batler or
laundress's beetle : or (and more probably) from the stirring round
of the buck when in the lie of the bucking tub, with the bucking-
stock. We still say 'drive a trade,' i. e. carry it on.

The Wassaile.

1. GIVE way, give way ye Gates, and win
    An easie blessing to your Bin,
 And Basket, by our entring in.

2. May both with manchet [3] stand repleat; [4]
 Your Larders too so hung with meat,
 That though a thousand, thousand eat;

3. Yet, ere twelve *Moons* shall whirl about
 Their silv'rie Spheres, ther's none may doubt,
 But more's sent in, then was serv'd out.   [*than*

4. Next, may your Dairies Prosper so,
 As that your Páns no Ebbe may know;
 But if they do, the more to flow,

5. Like to a solemne sober Stream
 Bankt all with Lillies and the Cream
 Of sweetest *Cow-slips* filling Them.

6. Then, may your Plants be prest with Fruit,
 Nor Bee, or Hive you have be mute;
 But sweetly sounding like a Lute.

7. Next may your Duck and teeming Hen
 Both to the Cocks-tread, say *Amen;*
 And for their two egs render ten.

---

[3] . = fine bread.   [4] = replete, filled.

8. Last, may your Harrows, Shares and Ploughes,
   Your Stacks, your Stocks,[5] your sweetest Mowes,[6]
   All prosper by our Virgin-vowes.

9. Alas! we blesse, but see none here,
   That brings us either Ale or Beere;
   In a drie-house all things are neere.[7]

10. Lets leave a longer Time to wait,
    Where Rust and Cobwebs, bind the gate;
    And all live here with *needy Fate.*

11. Where chimneys do for ever weepe,
    For want of warmth, and stomachs keepe
    With noise, the servants eyes from sleep.[8]

12. It is in vain to sing, or stay
    Our free-feet here; but we'l away:
    Yet to the Lares [9] this we'l say.

---

[5] = stooks or sheaves: a stook being a shock of corn containing 12 sheaves: 2 stooks a thrave.   [6] = laid up hay.

[7] A dry-house is a miserly not-giving house, the reference being not only to the want of drink, but to the dry hand which (teste Maria in All's Well) betokened a niggard in wealth and love. 'Neere' is seemingly an equivoque on 'ne'er' never, and near used as close-fisted.   [8] See Memorial-Introduction on this stanza.

[9] See Glossarial Index s. v.

13. The time will come, when you'l be sad
     And reckon this for fortune bad,
     T'ave lost the good ye might have had.

Upon a Lady Faire but fruitlesse.

TWICE has *Pudica* been a Bride, and led
     By holy *Hymen* to the Nuptiall Bed.
Two Youths sha's known thrice two, and twice 3
     yeares ;
Yet not a Lillie from the Bed appeares :
Nor will ; for why, *Pudica*, this may know,
Trees never beare, unlesse they first do blow.

How Springs came first.

THESE Springs were Maidens once that lov'd,
     But lost to that, they most approv'd :
My Story tels, by Love they were
Turn'd to these Springs, which we see here ;
The pretty whimpering that they make,
When of the Banks their leave they take ;
Tels yee but this, they are the same,
In nothing chang'd but in their name.

To Rosemary, and Baies.

M Y wooing's ended : now my weddings neere :
When Gloves are giving, *Guilded be you there.*[10]

Upon Skurffe.

S *KURFFE* by his Nine-bones [1] sweares, and well he
may,
All know a Fellon [2] eate the Tenth away.

Upon a Scarre in a Virgins Face.

'T IS Heresie in others : In your face
That Scarr's no *Schisme,*[3] but the *sign of grace.*

Upon his eye-sight failing him.

I BEGINNE to waine in sight ;
Shortly I shall bid goodnight :
Then no gazing more about,
When the Tapers once are out.

---

[10] Rosemary, &c., was gilded, or I suppose wrapped in gilded
paper for marriage festivities. See Glossarial Index s. v. He
speaks differently when this was his fate. See Memorial-Introduction.

[1] = fingers ?   [2] = a whitlow at the end of a finger affecting
the nail.   [3] = a pun on σχισμα rent, or division.

To his worthy Friend, M. Tho. Falconbirge.[4]

STAND with thy Graces forth, Brave man, and rise
   High with thine own *Auspitious Destinies :*
Nor leave the search, and proofe, till Thou canst find
These, or those ends, to which Thou wast design'd.
Thy lucky *Genius,* and thy guiding *Starre,*
Have made Thee prosperous in thy wayes, thus farre :
Nor will they leave Thee, till they both have shown
Thee to the World a *Prime* and *Publique One.*
Then, when Thou see'st thine Age all turn'd to gold,
Remember what thy *Herrick* Thee foretold,
When at the holy Threshold of thine house,
He Boded good-luck to thy Selfe and Spouse.
Lastly, be mindfull (when thou art grown great)
That Towrs high rear'd dread most the lightnings threat.
Whenas the humble Cottages not feare
The cleaving Bolt of Jove *the Thunderer.*[5]

Upon Julia's *haire fill'd with Dew.*

DEW sate on *Julia's* haire,
      And spangled too,
Like Leaves that laden are
      With trembling Dew :

---

[4] Not known.   [5] Some reminiscences of Horace : Od. ii. 10.

Or glitter'd to my sight,
 As when the Beames
Have their reflected light,
 Daunc't by the Streames.

Another on her.

HOW can I choose but love, and follow her,
 Whose shadow smels like milder *Pomander !*
How can I chuse but kisse her, whence do's come
The *Storax, Spiknard, Myrrhe,* and *Ladanum.*[6]

Losse from the least.

GREAT men by small meanes oft are overthrown :
 He's Lord of thy life, who contemnes his own.

Reward and punishments.

ALL things are open to these two events,
 Or to Rewards, or else to Punishments.

Shame, no Statist.

SHAME is a bad attendant to a State :
 He rents his Crown, That feares the Peoples hate.

---

[6] Ladanum (Lat.) or Labdanum—a fragrant gum.

To Sir Clisebie Crew.[7]

SINCE to th' Country first I came,
   I have lost my former flame:
And, methinks, I not inherit,
As I did, my ravisht spirit.
If I write a Verse, or two,
'Tis with very much ado;
In regard I want that Wine,
Which sho'd conjure up a line.
Yet, though now of Muse bereft,
I have still the manners left
For to thanke you (Noble Sir)
For those gifts you do conferre
Upon him, who only can
Be in Prose a *gratefull* man.

Upon himselfe.

1. I CO'D never love indeed;
      Never see mine own heart bleed:
   Never crucifie my life;
   Or for Widow, Maid, or Wife.

---

[7] See former notes on Crewe.

2. I co'd never seeke to please
One, or many Mistresses :
Never like their lips, to sweare
Oyle of Roses still smelt there.

3. I co'd never breake my sleepe,
Fold mine Armes, sob, sigh, or weep :
Never beg, or humbly wooe
With oathes, and lyes, (as others do.)

4. I co'd never walke alone ;
Put a shirt of sackcloth on :
Never keep a fast, or pray
For good luck in love (that day).

5. But have hitherto liv'd free,
As the aire that circles me :
And kept credit with my heart,
Neither broke i'th whole, or part.

Fresh Cheese and Cream.

WO'D yee have fresh Cheese and Cream ?
Iulia's Breast can give you them :
And if more ; Each *Nipple* cries,
To your *Cream*, her's *Strawberries.*

An Eclogue, or Pastorall between Endimion
Porter *and* Lycidas Herrick,
set and sung.

Endym. AH ! *Lycidas*, come tell me why
Thy whilome merry Oate[8]
By thee doth so neglected lye ;
And never purls[9] a note ?

2.   I prithee speake : *Lyc.* I will. *End.* Say on :
Lyc.   'Tis thou, and only thou,
That art the cause, *Endimion;*
End.   For Loves-sake, tell me how.

3. *Lyc.* In this regard, that thou do'st play
Upon another Plain :
And for a Rurall Roundelay,
Strik'st now a Courtly strain.

4.   Thou leav'st our Hills, our Dales, our Bowers,
Our finer fleecèd sheep :
(Unkind to us) to spend thine houres,
Where Shepheards sho'd not keep.

5.   I meane the Court : Let *Latmos* be
My lov'd *Endymions* Court ;

---

[8] =oaten reed or Pan-pipes.   [9] = pours forth.   See a very
full note on this word in my edition of Vaughan the Silurist s. n.

End. But I the Courtly State wo'd see :
Lyc.   Then see it in report.

6.   What ha's the Court to do with Swaines,
        Where *Phillis* is not known ?
    Nor do's it mind the Rustick straines
        Of us, or *Coridon.*

7.   Breake, if thou lov'st us, this delay ;
End.   Dear *Lycidas,* e're long,
    I vow by *Pan,* to come away
        And Pipe unto thy Song.

8.   Then *Jessimine,* with *Florabell ;*
        And dainty *Amarillis,*
    With handsome-handed *Drosomell*[1]
        Shall pranke thy Hooke with Lillies.

9. *Lyc.* Then *Tityrus,* and *Coridon,*
        And *Thyrsis,* they shall follow
    With all the rest ; while thou alone
        Shalt lead, like young *Apollo.*

10.   And till thou com'st, thy *Lycidas,*
        In every *Geniall* Cup,
    Shall write in Spice, *Endimion* 'twas
        That kept his Piping up.

[1] = honey-dew.

And my most luckie Swain, when I shall live to see
Endimions Moon to fill up full, remember me :
Mean time, let *Lycidas* have leave to Pipe to thee.

To a Bed of Tulips.

1. B RIGHT Tulips, we do know,
    You had your comming hither ;
    And Fading-time do's show,
    That Ye must quickly wither.

2. Your *Sister-hoods* may stay,
    And smile here for your houre ;
    But dye ye must away :
    Even as the meanest Flower.

3. Come Virgins then, and see
    Your frailties ; and bemone ye ;
    For lost like these, 'twill be,
    As Time had never known ye.

A Caution.

T HAT Love last long ; let it thy first care be
    To find a Wife, that is most fit for Thee.
Be She too wealthy, or too poore ; be sure,
Love in extreames, can never long endure.

To the Water Nymphs, drinking at the Fountain.

1. REACH, with your whiter hands, to me,
      Some Christall of the Spring ;
   And I, about the Cup shall see
      Fresh Lillies flourishing.

2. Or else sweet Nimphs do you but this ;
      To'th' Glasse your lips encline ;
   And I shall see by that one kisse,
      The Water turn'd to Wine.

To his Honoured Kinsman, Sir Richard Stone.[2]

TO this *white*[3] *Temple* of my *Heroes*, here
   Beset with stately Figures (every where)
Of such rare *Saint-ships*, who did here consume
Their lives in sweets, and left in death perfume.
Come, thou *Brave man !* And bring with Thee a Stone
Unto thine own *Edification*.
High are These Statues here, besides no lesse
Strong then the Heavens for everlastingnesse :   [*than*

---

[2] He was of Great Stukeley, co. Huntingdon, and was knighted at Huntingdon 14th March, 1641-2. He died in 1666: his Will was proved by his relict, Dame Elizabeth.

[3] See Glossarial Index s. v.

Where build aloft ; and being fixt by These,
Set up Thine own *eternall Images.*

Upon a Flie.

A GOLDEN Flie one shew'd to me,
   Clos'd in a Box of Yvorie :
Where both seem'd proud ; the Flie to have
His buriall in an yvory grave :
The yvorie tooke State to hold
A Corps as bright as burnisht gold.
One Fate had both ; both equall Grace ;
The Buried, and the Burying-place.
Not *Virgils Gnat,* to whom the Spring
All Flowers sent to'is burying ;
Not *Marshals* [4] *Bee,* which in a Bead
Of *Amber* [5] quick was burièd ;
Nor that fine Worme that do's interre
Her selfe i'th' *silken Sepulchre ;*
Nor my rare *Phil,*[6] that lately was
With Lillies Tomb'd up in a Glasse ;
More honour had, then this same *Flie ;*   [*than*
Dead, and closed up in Yvorie.

---

[4] Martial.   [5] =alive.   [6] Sparrow. H.

Upon Jack *and* Jill. *Epig.*

WHEN *Jill* complaines to *Jack* for want of meate ;
   Jack kisses *Jill,* and bids her freely eate :
Jill sayes, of what ? sayes *Jack,* on that sweet kisse,
Which full of Nectar and Ambrosia is,
The food of Poets ; so I thought sayes *Jill,*
That makes them looke so lanke, so Ghost-like still.
Let Poets feed on aire, or what they will ;
Let me feed full, till that I fart, sayes *Jill.*

To Julia.

JULIA, when thy *Herrick* dies,
   Close thou up thy Poets eyes :
And his last breath, let it be
Taken in by none but Thee.

To Mistresse Dorothy Parsons.

IF thou aske me (Deare) wherefore
   I do write of thee no more :
I must answer (Sweet) thy part
Lesse is here, then in my heart.   [*than*

Upon Parrat.

PARRAT protests 'tis he, and only he
   Can teach a man the *Art of memory :*

Believe him not ; for he forgot it quite,
Being drunke, who 'twas that Can'd his Ribs last night.

How he would drinke his Wine.

FILL me my Wine in Christall ; thus, and thus
    I see't in's *puris naturalibus :*
Unmixt.   I love to have it smirke and shine,   –
'Tis sin I know, 'tis sin to throtle Wine.
What Mad-man's he, that when it sparkles so,
Will coole his flames, or quench his fires with snow?

How Marigolds came yellow.

JEALOUS *Girles* these sometimes were,
    While they liv'd, or lasted here :
Turn'd to *Flowers*, still they be
Yellow, markt for Jealousie.

The broken Christall.

TO Fetch me Wine my *Lucia* went,
    Bearing a Christall *continent :*[7]
But making haste, it came to passe,
She brake in two the purer Glasse,
Then smil'd, and sweetly chid her speed ;
So with a blush, beshrew'd the deed.

[7] That in which anything is contained.

Precepts.

GOOD Precepts we must firmly hold,
By daily *Learning* we wax old.

To the right Honourable Edward *Earle* of
Dorset.[8]

IF I dare write to You, my Lord, who are,
Of your own selfe, a *Publick Theater*,
And sitting, see the wiles, wayes, walkes of wit,
And give a righteous judgement upon it,
What need I care, though some dislike me sho'd,
If *Dorset* say, what *Herrick* writes, is good?
We know y'are learn'd i'th' Muses, and no lesse
In our *State-sanctions*, deep, or bottomlesse.
Whose smile can make a Poet ; and your glance
Dash all bad Poems out of countenance.
So, that an Author needs no other Bayes
For Coronation, then Your onely[9] Praise.   [*than*
And no one mischief greater then your frown,
To null his Numbers, and to blast his Crowne.
Few live the life immortall.   He ensures
His Fame's long life, who strives to set up Yours.

[8] Edward Sackville, 4th Earl of Dorset : succeeded his brother
Richard in 1624.   He died in 1652.   [9] = praise alone.

Upon himself.

TH'art hence removing, (like a Shepherds Tent)
    And walk thou must the way that others went
Fall thou must first, then rise to life with These;
Markt in thy Book for faithfull Witnesses.

Hope well and Have well : or,
Faire after Foule weather.

WHAT though the Heaven be lowring now,
    And look with a contracted brow?
We shall discover, by and by,
A Repurgation of the Skie :
And when those clouds away are driven,
Then will appeare a cheerfull Heaven.

Upon Love.

1. I HELD Love's head while it did ake ;
      But so it chanc't to be ;
  The cruell paine did his forsake,
      And forthwith came to me.

2. Ai me ! how shal my griefe be stil'd ?
      Or where else shall we find
  One like to me, who must be kill'd
      For being too-too-kind ?

To his Kinswoman, Mrs. Penelope Wheeler.[10]

NEXT is your lot (Faire) to be number'd one,
  Here, in my Book's Canonization :
Late you come in ; but you a Saint shall be,
In Chiefe, in this Poetick Liturgie.

Another upon her.

FIRST, for your shape, the curious cannot shew
  Any one part that's dissonant in you:
And 'gainst your chast behaviour there's no Plea,
Since you are knowne to be *Penelope.*
Thus faire and cleane you are, although there be
A mighty strife 'twixt Forme [1] *and Chastitie.*

Kissing and bussing.

KISSING and bussing[2] differ both in this ;
  We busse our Wantons, but our Wives we kisse.

Crosse and Pile.

FAIRE and foule dayes trip Crosse and Pile;[3] The
  faire
Far lesse in number, then our foule dayes are.   [*than*

---

[10] See Memorial-Introduction.   [1] =beauty (Latin *forma*).
[2] =slavering kiss, but this distinction, if ever it existed, was not kept up, for ' buss ' was and is still used simply as a kiss.
[3] =tails and heads.

To the Lady Crew, *upon the death of her Child.*[4]

WHY, Madam, will ye longer weep,
　　Whenas your Baby's lull'd asleep ?
And (pretty Child) feeles now no more
Those paines it lately felt before.
All now is silent ; groanes are fled :
Your Child lyes still, yet is not dead :
But rather like a flower hid here
To spring againe another yeare.

His Winding-sheet.

COME thou, who art the Wine, and wit
　　　　Of all I've writ :
The Grace, the Glorie, and the best
　　　　Piece of the rest.
Thou art of what I did intend
　　　　The All, and End.
And what was made, was made to meet
　　　　Thee, thee my sheet.
Come then, and be to my chast side
　　　　Both Bed, and Bride.

---

[4] See before.　Frances, d. of Sir Clipsby Crewe, and Jane his wife, was born at Crewe 27th July, **1631** : died 4th Feb. **1637-8**, and was buried in Westminster Abbey.

We two (as Reliques left) will have
  One Rest, one Grave.
And, hugging close, we will not feare
  Lust entring here
Where all Desires are dead, or cold
  As is the mould :
And all Affections are forgot,
  Or Trouble not.
Here, here the Slaves and Pris'ners be
  From Shackles free :
And Weeping Widowes long opprest
  Doe here find rest.
The wrongèd Client ends his Lawes
  Here, and his Cause.
Here those long suits of Chancery lie
  Quiet, or die :
And all Star-chamber-Bils doe cease,
  Or hold their peace.
Here needs no Court for our Request,
  Where all are best ;
All wise ; all equall ; and all just
  Alike i'th' dust.
Nor need we here to feare the frowne
  Of Court, or Crown.
Where Fortune bears no sway o're things
  There all are Kings.

In this securer place we'l keep,
    As lull'd asleep ;
Or for a little time we'l lye,
    As Robes laid by ;
To be another day re-worne,
    Turn'd, but not torn :
Or like old Testaments ingrost,
    Lockt up, not lost :
And for a while lye here conceal'd,
    To be reveal'd
Next, at that great Platonick yeere,[5]
    And then meet here.

To Mistresse Mary Willand.[6]

ONE more by Thee, Love, and Desert have sent,
    T' enspangle this expansive Firmament.
O Flame of Beauty ! come, appeare, appeare
A Virgin Taper, ever shining here.

Change gives content.

WHAT now we like, anon we disapprove :
    The new successor drives away old Love.

[5] According to Plato in Timæus, the period in which the eight stellar circles complete their rotation round the axis of the Kosmos, and return to the same position.   [6] Unknown.

Upon Magot *a frequenter of Ordinaries.*

MAGOT frequents those houses of good-cheere,
　　Talkes most, eates most, of all the Feeders
　　　　there.
He raves through leane, he rages through the fat ;
(What gets the master of the Meal by that ?)
He who with talking can devoure so much,
How wo'd he eate, were not his hindrance such ?

On himselfe.

BORNE I was to meet with Age,
　　And to walke Life's pilgrimage.
Much I know of Time is spent,
Tell I can't, what's Resident.
Howsoever, cares, adue ;
Ile have nought to say to you :
But Ile spend my comming houres,
Drinking wine, & crown'd with flowres.

Fortune favours.

FORTUNE did never favour one
　　Fully, without exception ;
Though free she be, ther's something yet
Still wanting to her Favourite.

To Phillis *to love, and live with him.*

LIVE, live with me, and thou shalt see
    The pleasures Ile prepare for thee :
What sweets the Country can afford
Shall blesse thy Bed, and blesse thy Board.
The soft sweet Mosse shall be thy bed,
With crawling Woodbine over-spread :
By which the silver-shedding [7] streames
Shall gently melt thee into dreames.
Thy clothing next, shall be a Gowne
Made of the Fleeces purest Downe.
The tongues of Kids shall be thy meate ;
Their Milke thy drinke ; and thou shalt eate
The Paste of Filberts for thy bread
With Cream of Cowslips butterèd :
Thy Feasting-Tables shall be Hills
With *Daisies* spread, and *Daffadils* ;
Where thou shalt sit, and *Red-brest* by,
For meat, shall give thee melody.
Ile give thee Chaines and Carkanets [8]
Of *Primroses* and *Violets.*
A Bag and Bottle thou shalt have ;
That richly wrought, and This as brave ;

---

[7] See Glossarial Index s. v.   [8] Ibid.

So that as either shall expresse
The Wearer's no meane Shepheardesse.
At Sheering-times, and yearely Wakes,
When *Themilis* his pastime makes,
There thou shalt be ; and be the wit,
Nay more, the Feast, and grace of it.
On Holy-dayes, when Virgins meet
To dance the Heyes [9] with nimble feet ;
Thou shalt come forth, and then appeare
The *Queen of Roses* for that yeere.
And having danc't ('bove all the best)
Carry the Garland from the rest.
In Wicker-baskets Maids shal bring
To thee, (my dearest Shepharling) [1]
The blushing Apple, bashfull Peare,
And shame-fac't Plum, (all simp'ring [2] there) :
Walk in the Groves, and thou shalt find
The name of *Phillis* in the Rind
Of every straight, and smooth-skin tree ;
Where kissing that, Ile twice kisse thee.
To thee a Sheep-hook I will send,
Be-pranckt with Ribbands, to this end,

---

[9] A dance : see Sir John Davies' "Orchestra."
[1] A diminutive of shepherdess.   [2] See Glossarial Index s. v.

This, this alluring Hook might be
Lesse for to catch a sheep, then me.   [*than*
Thou shalt have Possets, Wassails fine,
Not made of Ale, but spicèd Wine ;
To make thy Maids and selfe free mirth,
All sitting neer the glitt'ring Hearth.
Thou sha't have Ribbands, Roses, Rings,
Gloves, Garters, Stockings, Shooes, and Strings
Of winning Colours, that shall move
Others to Lust, but me to Love.
These (nay) and more, thine own shal be,
If thou wilt love, and live with me.

.

To his Kinswoman, Mistresse
Susanna Herrick.[3]

WHEN I consider (Dearest) thou dost stay
        But here awhile, to languish and decay ;
Like to these Garden-glories, which here be
The Flowrie-sweet resemblances of Thee :
With griefe of heart, methinks, I thus doe cry,
Wo'd thou hadst ne'r been born, or might'st not die.

[3] See Memorial-Introduction.

/

Upon Mistresse Susanna Southwell
her cheeks.[4]

R ARE are thy cheeks *Susanna*, which do show
Ripe Cherries smiling, while that others blow.

Upon her Eyes.

C LEERE are her eyes,
Like purest Skies.
Discovering from thence
A Babie [5] there
That turns each Sphere,
Like an Intelligence.

Upon her feet.[6]

H ER pretty feet
Like snailes did creep
A little out, and then,
As if they started at Bo-Beep,
Did soon draw in agen.

[4] Doubtless a d. of Sir Thomas Southwell, as before.
[5] See Glossarial Index s. v.
[6] See Memorial-Introduction on this in relation to Suckling.

To his honoured friend, Sir John Mynts.[7]

FOR civill, cleane, and circumcisèd wit,
     And for the comely carriage of it;
Thou art The Man, the onely Man best known,
Markt for the *True-wit* of a Million :
From whom we'l reckon.   Wit came in, but since
The *Calculation* of thy Birth, *Brave Mince.*

Upon his gray haires.

FLY me not, though I be gray,
     Lady, this I know you'l say;
Better look the Roses red,
When with white comminglèd.
Black your haires are; mine are white;
This begets the more delight,
When things meet most opposite :
As in Pictures we descry,
Venus standing *Vulcan* by.

[7] The well-known Comptroller and Commissioner of the Navy, of whom Pepys has so much to say in his Diary.   He was knighted at Dover 15th Feb., 1641-2, being the Vice-Admiral.   The right spelling seems to have been Mennes—as he so signed his name.   He died in 1671.

Accusation.

IF Accusation onely can draw blood,
   None shall be guiltlesse, be he n'er so good.

Pride allowable in Poets.

AS thou deserv'st, be proud ; then gladly let
   The Muse give thee the Delphick Coronet.

A Vow to Minerva.

GODDESSE, I begin an Art ;
   Come thou in, with thy best part,
For to make the Texture lye
Each way smooth and civilly :[8]
And a broad-fac't Owle shall be
Offer'd up with Vows to Thee.

On Jone.

JONE wo'd go tel her haires ; and well she might,
   Having but seven in all ; three black, foure white.

Upon Letcher.   *Epig.*

LETCHER was Carted first about the streets,
   For false Position in his neighbours sheets :

---

[8] = not disordered.

Next, hang'd for Theeving : Now the people say,
His Carting was the *Prologue* to this Play.

Upon Dundrige.

D UNDRIGE his Issue hath ; but is not styl'd
For all his Issue, Father of one Child.[9]

To Electra.

1. 'TIS Ev'ning, my Sweet,
     And dark ; let us meet ;
Long time w'ave here been a-toying :
     And never, as yet,
     That season co'd get,
Wherein t'ave had an enjoying.

2. For pitty or shame,
     Then let not Love's flame,
Be ever and ever a-spending ;
     Since now to the Port
     The path is but short ;
And yet our way has no ending.

3. Time flyes away fast ;
     Our houres doe waste :

[9] Issue = an old sore, or one made to prevent other illness.

The while we never remember,
　　How soone our life, here,
　　Growes old with the yeere,
That dyes with the next *December.*

Discord not disadvantageous.

FORTUNE no higher Project can devise,
　　Then to sow Discord 'mongst the Enemies.

Ill Government.

PREPOSTEROUS is that Government, (and rude)
When Kings obey the wilder Multitude.

To Marygolds.

GIVE way, and be ye ravisht by the Sun,
　　(And hang the head whenas the Act is done)
Spread as He spreads ; wax lesse as He do's wane ;
And as He shuts, close up to Maids[1] again.

To Dianeme.

GIVE me one kisse,
　　And no more ;
　　If so be, this
　　Makes you poore ;

[1] = as in your maiden budding time.

To enrich you,
    Ile restore
For that one, two
    Thousand score.

To Julia, *the* Flaminica Dialis,[2]
    or, Queen-Priest.

THOU know'st, my *Julia*, that it is thy turne
    This Mornings Incense to prepare, and burne.
The Chaplet, and *Inarculum*[3] here be,
With the white[4] Vestures, all attending Thee.
This day, the *Queen-Priest*, thou art made t'appease
Love for our very-many Trespasses.
One chiefe transgression is among the rest,
Because with Flowers her Temple was not drest :
The next, because her Altars did not shine
With daily Fyers : The last, neglect of Wine :
For which, her wrath is gone forth to consume
Us all, unlesse preserv'd by thy Perfume.
Take then thy Censer ; Put in Fire, and thus,
O *Pious-Priestresse !* make a Peace for us.
For our neglect, Love did our Death decree,
That we escape.   *Redemption comes by Thee.*

[2] = wife of the arch-priest of Jupiter.
[3] A twig of a pomgranat, which the queen-priest did use to wear
on her head at sacrificing. H.   [4] See Glossarial Index s. v.

Anacreontike.

BORN I was to be old,
    And for to die here :
After that, in the mould
    Long for to lye here.
But before that day comes,
    Still I be Bousing ;
For I know, in the Tombs
    There's no Carousing.

Meat without mirth.

EATEN I have ; and though I had good cheere,
    I did not sup, because no friends were there.
Where Mirth and Friends are absent when we Dine
Or Sup, there wants the Incense and the Wine.

Large Bounds doe but bury us.

ALL things o'r-rul'd are here by Chance ;
    The greatest mans Inheritance.
Whereere the luckie Lot doth fall,
Serves but for place of Buriall.

Upon Ursley.

URSLEY, she thinks those Velvet Patches grace
    The Candid [5] Temples of her comely face :

[5] **See Glossarial Index s. v.**

But he will say, whoe'r those Circlets seeth,
They be but signs of *Ursleys* hollow teeth.

An Ode to Sir Clipsebie Crew.[6]

1. HERE we securely live, and eate
      The Creame of meat ;
   And keep eternal fires,
   By which we sit, and doe Divine
         As Wine
      And Rage inspires.

2. If full we charme ; then call upon
      Anacreon
   To grace the frantick Thyrse :[7]
   And having drunk, we raise a shout
         Throughout
      To praise his Verse.

3. Then cause we *Horace* to be read,
      Which sung, or seyd,
   A Goblet, to the brim,
   Of Lyrick Wine, both swell'd and crown'd,

---

[6] See previous poems to and of him.   [7] See Glossarial Index s. v.

A Round[8]
We quaffe to him.

4. Thus, thus, we live, and spend the houres
In Wine and Flowers :
And make the frollick yeere,
The Month, the Week, the instant[9] Day
To stay
The longer here.

5. Come then, brave Knight, and see the Cell
Wherein I dwell ;
And my Enchantments too ;
Which Love and noble freedome is ;
And this
Shall fetter you.

6. Take Horse, and come ; or be so kind,
To send your mind
(Though but in Numbers few)
And I shall think I have the heart,
Or part
Of *Clipseby Crew.*

[8] See Glossarial Index s. v.: but here it must mean a health round, drank from one to the other, as the loving-cup still is, where it begins and ends with the same person. [9] See Glossarial Index s. v.

To his worthy Kinsman, Mr.
Stephen Soame.[10]

NOR is my Number full, till I inscribe
    Thee sprightly *Soame*, one of my righteous
    Tribe :
A Tribe of one Lip ; Leven,[1] and of One
Civil[2] Behaviour, and Religion.
A Stock of Saints ; where ev'ry one doth weare
A stole of white, (and Canonizèd here)
Among which Holies, be Thou ever known,
Brave Kinsman, markt out with the whiter[3] stone :
Which seals Thy Glorie ; since I doe prefer
Thee here in my eternall Calender.

To his Tomb-maker.

GO I must ; when I am gone,
    Write but this upon my Stone ;
Chaste I liv'd, without a wife,
That's the Story of my life.
Strewings need none, every flower
Is in this word, Batchelour.

---

[10] Sir Thomas Soame had a brother Stephen, and a son Stephen.
[1] = leaven [i. e. of one leaven.]   [2] = dignified.
[3] See Glossarial Index s. v.

Great Spirits supervive.

OUR mortall parts may wrapt in Seare-cloths lye :
Great Spirits never with their bodies dye.

None free from fault.

OUT of the world he must, who once comes in :
No man exempted is from Death, or sinne.

Upon himselfe being buried.

LET me sleep this night away,
Till the Dawning of the day :
Then at th' opening of mine eyes,
I, and all the world shall rise.

Pitie to the prostrate.

'TIS worse then barbarous cruelty to show   [*than*
No part of pitie on a conquer'd foe.

Way in a crowd.

ONCE on a Lord-Mayors day, in Cheapside, when
Skulls co'd not well passe through that scum of
men
For quick dispatch, *Sculls* made no longer stay,
Then but to breath, and every one gave way :   [*than*

For as he breath'd, the People swore from thence
A Fart flew out, or a *Sir-reverence.*

His Content in the Country.

HERE, here I live with what my Board,
    Can with the smallest cost afford.
Though ne'r so mean the Viands be,
They well content my *Prew* and me.
Or Pea, or Bean, or Wort,[4] or Beet,
Whatever comes, content makes sweet :
Here we rejoyce, because no Rent
We pay for our poore Tenement :
Wherein we rest, and never feare
The Landlord, or the Usurer.
The Quarter-day do's ne'r affright
Our Peacefull slumbers in the night.
We eate our own, and batten[5] more,
Because we feed on no mans score :
But pitie those, whose flanks grow great,
Swel'd with the Lard of others meat.
We blesse our Fortunes, when we see
Our own belovèd privacie :
And like our living, where w'are known
To very few, or else to none.

[4] =cabbage-kind.   [5] =fatten.

The Credit of the Conquerer.

HE who commends the vanquisht, speaks the
    Power,
And glorifies the worthy Conquerer.

On himselfe.

SOME parts may perish; dye thou canst not all :
    The most of Thee shall scape the funerall.

Upon one-ey'd Broomsted.   Epig.

BROOMSTED a lamenesse got by cold and Beere ;
    And to the *Bath* went, to be curèd there :
His feet were helpt, and left his Crutch behind :
But home return'd, as he went forth, halfe blind.

The Fairies.

IF ye will with *Mab* find grace,
    Set each Platter in his place :
Rake the Fier up, and get
Water in, ere Sun be set.
Wash your Pailes, and clense your Dairies ;
Sluts are loathsome to the Fairies :
Sweep your house : Who doth not so,
Mab will pinch her by the toe.

To his Honoured friend, M. John Weare, Councellour.[6]

DID I or love, or could I others draw
    To the indulgence of the rugged Law :
The first foundation of that zeale sho'd be
By Reading all her *Paragraphs* in Thee.
Who dost so fitly with the Lawes unite,
As if You Two, were one *Hermophrodite :*
Nor courts thou Her because she's well attended
With wealth, but for those ends she was entended :
Which were, (and still her offices are known)
Law is to give to ev'ry one his owne.
To shore [7] the Feeble up, against the strong ;
To shield the Stranger, and the Poore from wrong :
This was the Founders grave and good intent,
To keepe the out-cast in his Tenement :
To free the Orphan from that Wolfe-like-man,
Who is his *Butcher* more then *Guardian.*   [*than*
To drye the Widowes teares ; and stop her Swoones,
By pouring Balme and Oyle into her wounds.
This was the old way ; and 'tis yet thy course,
To keep those pious Principles in force.

---

[6] Apparently unknown now.   [7] = prop.

Modest I will be ; but one word Ile say
(Like to a sound that's vanishing away)
Sooner the in-side of thy hand shall grow
Hispèd,[8] and hairie, ere thy Palm shall know
A *Postern-bribe*[9] tooke, or a *Forkèd-Fee*[1]
To fetter Justice, when She might be free.
Eggs Ile not shave: But yet, brave man, if I
Was destin'd forth to golden Soveraignty :
A Prince I'de be, that I might Thee preferre
To be my Counsell both, and Chanceller.

The Watch.

MAN is a Watch, wound up at first, but never
　　Wound up again : Once down, He's down for
　　　ever.
The Watch once downe, all motions then do cease ;
And Mans Pulse stopt, *All Passions sleep in Peace.*

Lines have their Linings, and Bookes their Buckram.

AS in our clothes, so likewise he who lookes,
　　Shall find much farcing Buckram[2] in our Books.

---

[8] = Latin hispidus, rough.　　[9] = a back-door or secret bribe.
[1] Query—a fee from the other side as well as from his client ?
[2] See Glossarial Index s. v.

Art above Nature, to Julia.

WHEN I behold a Forrest spread
    With silken trees upon thy head ;
And when I see that other Dresse
Of flowers set in comlinesse :
When I behold another grace
In the ascent of curious Lace,
Which like a Pinacle doth shew
The top, and the top-gallant[3] too.
Then, when I see thy Tresses bound
Into an Ovall, square, or round ;
And knit in knots far more then I   [*than*
Can tell by tongue ; or true-love tie :
Next, when those Lawnie Filmes I see
Play with a wild civility : [4]
And all those airie silks to flow,
Alluring me, and tempting so :
I must confesse, mine eye and heart
Dotes less on Nature, then on Art.   [*than*

Upon Sibilla.

WITH paste of Almonds, *Syb* her hands doth
    scoure ;
Then gives it to the children to devoure.

---

[3] = highest sail.   [4] See Glossarial Index s. v.

In Cream she bathes her thighs (more soft then silk) [*than*
Then to the poore she freely gives the milke.

Upon his kinswoman, Mistresse Bridget Herrick.[5]

SWEET *Bridget* blusht, & therewithall,
   Fresh blossoms from her cheekes did falL
I thought at first 'twas but a dream,
Till after I had handled them ;
And smelt them, then they smelt to me,
As Blossomes of the *Almond* tree.

Upon Love.

1. I PLAID with Love, as with the fire
   The wanton Satyre did ;
Nor did I know, or co'd descry
   What under there was hid.

2. That Satyre he but burnt his lips ;
   (But min's the greater smart)
For kissing Loves dissembling chips,
   The fire scortcht my heart.[6]

Upon a comely, and curious Maide.

IF men can say that beauty dyes ;
   Marbles will sweare that here it lyes.

[5] See Memorial-Introduction.   [6] Ibid.

If Reader then thou canst forbeare,
In publique loss to shed a Teare :
The Dew of griefe upon this stone
Will tell thee *Pitie* thou hast none.

Upon the losse of his Finger.

ONE of the five straight branches of my hand
    Is lopt already ;[7] and the rest but stand
Expecting when to fall : which soon will be ;
First dyes the Leafe, the Bough next, next the Tree.

Upon Irene.

ANGRY if *Irene* be
    But a Minutes life with me :
Such a fire I espie
Walking in and out her eye,
As at once I freeze, and frie.[8]

Upon Electra's *Teares.*

UPON her cheekes she wept, and from those
    showers
Sprang up a sweet *Nativity* of Flowres.

[7] See Randolph in Memorial-Introduction on a like loss.
[8] See Glossarial Index s. v.

Upon Tooly.

THE Eggs of Pheasants wrie-nosed *Tooly* sells ;
　But ne'r so much as licks the speckled shells :
Only, if one prove addled, that he eates
With superstition, (as the Cream of meates.)
The Cock and Hen he feeds ; but not a bone
He ever pickt (as yet) of any one.

A Hymne to the Graces.

WHEN I love, (as some have told,
　Love I shall when I am old)
O ye Graces ! Make me fit
For the welcoming of it.
Clean my Roomes, as Temples be,
T' entertain that Deity.
Give me words wherewith to wooe,
Suppling and successefull too :
Winning postures ; and withall,
Manners each way musicall :
Sweetnesse to allay my sowre
And unsmooth behaviour.
For I know you have the skill
Vines to prune, though not to kill,
And of any wood ye see,
You can make a *Mercury.*

To Silvia.

NO more my *Silvia*, do I mean to pray
      For those good dayes that ne'r will come away.
I want beliefe ; O gentle *Silvia*, be
The patient Saint, and send up vowes for me.

Upon Blanch.   *Epig*.

I HAVE seen many Maidens to have haire ;
      Both for their comely need, and some to spare :
But *Blanch* has not so much upon her head,
As to bind up her chaps when she is dead.

Upon Vmber.   *Epig*.

U *MBER* was painting of a Lyon fierce,
      And working it, by chance from *Umbers* Erse
Flew out a crack, so mighty, that the Fart,
(As *Umber* sweares) did make his Lyon start.

The Poet hath lost his pipe.

I CANNOT pipe as I was wont to do,
      Broke is my Reed, hoarse is my singing too
My wearied Oat[9] Ile hang upon the Tree,
And give it to the *Silvan Deitie*.

---

[9] = oaten pipe.

True Friendship.

WILT thou my true Friend be ?
  Then love not mine, but me.

The Apparition of his Mistresse
calling him to Elizium.

Desunt nonnulla ————

COME then, and like two Doves with silv'rie wings,
  Let our soules flie to' the' shades, where ever
    springs
Sit smiling in the Meads ; where Balme and Oile,
Roses and Cassia crown the untill'd soyle.
Where no disease raignes, or infection comes
To blast the Aire, but *Amber-greece*[1] and *Gums*.
This, that, and ev'ry Thicket doth transpire
More sweet, then *Storax* from the hallowed fire : [*than*
Where ev'ry tree a wealthy issue beares
Of fragrant Apples, blushing Plums, or Peares :
And all the shrubs, with sparkling spangles, shew
Like Morning-Sun-shine tinsilling the dew.
Here in green Meddowes sits eternall May,
Purfling[2] the Margents,[3] while perpetuall Day

---

[1] See Glossarial Index s. v.
[2] = with gold thread or embroidery.   [3] = margins : " By the beached margent of the sea " (Mid. N. Dream ii. 1).

So double gilds the Aire, as that no night
Can ever rust th'Enamel of the light.
Here, naked Younglings, handsome Striplings run
Their Goales for Virgins kisses ; which when done,
Then unto Dancing forth the learnèd Round
Commixt they meet, with endlesse Roses crown'd.
And here we'l sit on Primrose-banks, and see
Love's *Chorus* led by *Cupid ;* and we'l be
Two loving followers too unto the Grove,
Where Poets sing the stories of our love.
There thou shalt hear Divine *Musæus* sing
Of *Hero*, and *Leander ;* then Ile bring
Thee to the Stand, where honour'd *Homer* reades
His *Odisees*, and his high *Iliades.*
About whose Throne the crowd of Poets throng
To heare the incantation of his tongue :
To *Linus*,[4] then to *Pindar ;* and that done,
Ile bring thee *Herrick* to *Anacreon*,
Quaffing his full-crown'd bowles of burning Wine,
And in his Raptures speaking Lines of Thine,
Like to His subject ; and as his Frantick-
Looks, shew him truly *Bacchanalian* like,

[4] A mythical poet (Diodorus iii. 66). See on the others our Me
morial-Introduction.

Besmear'd with Grapes ; welcome he shall thee
      thither,
Where both may rage, both drink and dance to-
      gether.
Then stately *Virgil*, witty *Ovid*, by
Whom faire *Corinna* sits, and doth comply [5]
With Yvorie wrists, his Laureat head, and steeps
His eye in dew of kisses, while he sleeps.
Then soft *Catullus*, sharp-fang'd *Martial*,
And towring *Lucan, Horace, Juvenal*,
And Snakie *Perseus*, these, and those, whom Rage
(Dropt from [6] the jarres of heaven) fill'd t'engage
All times unto their frenzies ; Thou shalt there
Behold them in a spacious Theater.
Among which glories, (crown'd with sacred Bayes,
And flatt'ring Ivie) Two recite their Plaies,
Beumont and *Fletcher*, Swans, to whom all eares
Listen, while they (like Syrens in their Spheres)
Sing their *Evadne ;* and still more for thee
There yet remaines to know, then thou can'st see [*than*
By glim'ring of a fancie : Doe but come,
And there Ile shew thee that capacious roome

  [5] = complere : infold.
  [6] Misprinted ' for ' in original : corrected to ' from,' i. e. heavenly
rages.

In which thy Father *Johnson* now is plac't,
As in a Globe of Radiant fire,[7] and grac't
To be in that Orbe crown'd (that doth include
Those Prophets of the former Magnitude)
And he one chiefe ; But harke, I heare the Cock,
(The Bell-man of the night) proclaime the clock
Of late struck one ; and now I see the prime
Of Day break from the pregnant East, 'tis time
I vanish ; more I had to say ;
But Night determines[8] here, Away.

Life is the Bodies Light.

LIFE is the Bodies light ; which once declining,
    Those crimson clouds i'th'cheeks & lips leave
        shining.
Those counter-changèd *Tabbies*[9] in the ayre,
(The Sun once set) all of one colour are.
So, when Death comes, *Fresh tinctures* lose their
        place,
And dismall Darknesse then doth smutch[1] the face.

---

[7] See Memorial-Introduction for Giles Fletcher and Milton on
' a Globe of Radiant fire.'
[8] = terminates.
[9] = tabby, a wavy or wave-figured silk : here put for the clouds.
[1] = smudge.

Upon Urles. *Epig.*

U*RLES* had the Gout so, that he co'd not stand ;
  Then from his Feet, it shifted to his Hand :
When 'twas in's Feet, his Charity was small ;
Now tis in's Hand, he gives no Almes at all.

Upon Franck.

F*RANCK* ne'r wore silk she sweares ; but I reply,
  She now weares silk to hide her blood-shot eye.

Love lightly pleased.

L ET faire or foule my Mistresse be,
    Or low, or tall, she pleaseth me :
Or let her walk, or stand, or sit,
The posture hers, I'm pleas'd with it.
Or let her tongue be still, or stir,
Gracefull is ev'ry thing from her.
Or let her Grant, or else Deny,
My Love will fit each Historie.

The Primrose.

A SKE me why I send you here
    This sweet *Infanta*[2] of the yeere ?

[2] = Princess.

Aske me why I send to you
This Primrose, thus bepearl'd with dew ?
I will whisper to your eares,
The sweets of Love are mixt with tears.

2.   Ask me why this flower do's show
So yellow-green, and sickly too ?
Ask me why the stalk is weak
And bending (yet it doth not break ?)
I will answer, These discover
What fainting hopes are in a Lover.

The Tythe. To the Bride.

IF nine times you your Bride-groome kisse ;
The tenth you know the Parsons is.
Pay then your Tythe ; and doing thus,
Prove in your Bride-bed numerous.
If children you have ten, Sir *John*[3]
Won't for his tenth part ask you one.

A Frolick.

BRING me my Rose-buds, Drawer come ;
So, while I thus sit crown'd ;
Ile drink the aged *Cœcubum,*[4]
Untill the roofe turne round.

---

[3] = the parson, as his tythe.   [4] = a Campanian wine

Change common to all.

ALL things subjected are to Fate ;
   Whom this Morne sees most fortunate,
The Ev'ning sees in poore estate.

To Julia.

THE Saints-bell calls ; and, *Julia*, I must read
   The Proper Lessons for the Saints now dead :
To grace which Service, *Julia*, there shall be
One *Holy Collect*, said or sung for Thee.
Dead when thou art, Deare *Julia*, thou shalt have
A *Tentrall*[5] sung by Virgins o're thy Grave :
Meanetime we two will sing the Dirge of these ;
Who dead, deserve our best remembrances.

No Luck in Love.

1. I DOE love I know not what ;
   Sometimes this, & sometimes that :
All conditions I aime at.

2. But, as lucklesse, I have yet
Many shrewd disasters met,
To gaine her whom I wo'd get.

[5] = trentall: see Glossarial Index s. v.

3. Therefore now Ile love no more,
   As I've doted heretofore :
   He who must be, shall be poore.[6]

In the darke none dainty.

NIGHT hides our thefts; all faults then pardon'd
      be :
All are alike faire, when no spots we see.
Lais and *Lucrece,* in the nighttime are
Pleasing alike; alike both singular :
Jone, and my lady have at that time one,
One and the selfe-same priz'd complexion.
Then please alike the Pewter and the Plate ;
The chosen *Rubie,* and the *Reprobate.*

A charme, or an allay[7] for Love.

IF so be a Toad be laid
   In a Sheeps-skin newly flaid,
And that ty'd to man 'twil sever
Him and his affections ever.[8]

Upon a free Maid, with a foule breath.

YOU say you'l kiss me, and I thanke you for it:
   But stinking breath, I do as hell abhorre it.

---

[6] = He who must be [poor] shall be.
[7] = soothing cure.   [8] Folk-lore.

Upon Coone.   *Epig.*

HAT is the reason *Coone* so dully smels ?
His Nose is over-cool'd with Isicles.

To his Brother in Law Master John
Wingfield.[9]

FOR being comely, consonant,[1] and free
    To most of men, but most of all to me :
For so decreeing, that thy clothes expence
Keepes still within a just circumference :
Then for contriving so to loade thy Board,
As that the Messes ne'r o'r-laid the Lord :
Next for Ordaining, that thy words not swell
To any one unsober *syllable.*
These I co'd praise thee for beyond another,
Wert thou a *Winckfield* onely, not a Brother.

The Head-ake.

1. MY head doth ake,
        O *Sappho !* take
    Thy fillit,
    And bind the paine ;
    Or bring some bane
        To kill it.

---

[9] See Memorial-Introduction.   [1] = agreeable.

.

2. But lessse that part,
    Then my poore heart,
        Now is sick :
    One kisse from thee
    Will counsell be,
        And Physick.

On himselfe.

LIVE by thy Muse thou shalt ; when others die,
    Leaving no Fame to long Posterity :
When Monarchies trans-shifted are, and gone ;
Here shall endure thy vast Dominion.

Upon a Maide.

HENCE a blessed soule is fled,
    Leaving here the body dead :
Which (since here they can't combine)
For the Saint, we'l keep the Shrine.

Upon Spalt.

OF Pushes[2] *Spalt* has such a knottie race,
    He needs a Tucker[3] for to burle[4] his face.

---

[2] Push = a pimple or little pock.   [3] = a Fuller of cloth.
[4] = to dress cloth as does a Fuller, removing the knots.

Of Horne *a Comb-maker.*

H ORNE sells to others teeth ; but has not one
To grace his own Gums, or of Box,[5] or bone.

Upon the troublesome times.

1.   O ! Times most bad,
        Without the scope
        Of hope
    Of better to be had !

2.   Where shall I goe,
        Or whither run
        To shun
    This publique overthrow?

3.   No places are
        (This I am sure)
        Secure
    In this our wasting Warre.

4.   Some storms w'ave past ;
        Yet we must all
        Down fall,
    And perish at the last.

[5] = box-wood.

Cruelty base in Commanders.

NOTHING can be more loathsome, then to see [*than*
　　Power conjoyn'd with Natures *Crueltie.*

Upon a sowre-breath Lady.　Epig.

FIE, (quoth my Lady) what a stink is here?
　　When 'twas her breath that was the *Carrionere.*[6]

Upon Lucia.

I ASKT my *Lucia* but a kisse;
　　And she with scorne deny'd me this:
Say then, how ill sho'd I have sped,
Had I then askt her Maidenhead?

Little and loud.

LITTLE you are; for Womans sake be proud;
　　For my sake next, (though little) *be not loud.*

Ship-wrack.

HE, who has suffer'd Ship-wrack, feares to saile
　　Upon the Seas, though with a gentle gale.

---

[6] = carrioneer, as we would spell it—a coinage for the bearer of carrion—her breath brought or carried it. There is also a wicked and ungallant pun on carrion = her breath stunk like carrion.

Paines without profit.

A LONG-lifes-day I've taken paines
  For very little, or no gaines :
The Ev'ning's come ; here now Ile stop,
And work no more ; but shut up Shop.

To his Booke.

BE bold, my Booke, nor be abasht, or feare
  The cutting Thumb-naile, or the Brow severe.
But by the *Muses* sweare, all here is good,
If but well read ; or ill read, understood.

His Prayer to Ben. Johnson.

1. WHEN I a Verse shall make,
      Know I have praid thee,
   For old *Religions* sake,
   Saint *Ben* to aide me.

2. Make the way smooth for me,
   When I, thy *Herrick*,
   Honouring thee, on my knee
   Offer my *Lyrick*.

3. Candles Ile give to thee,
   And a new Altar ;
   And thou Saint *Ben*, shalt be
   Writ in my *Psalter*.

Poverty and Riches.

GIVE *Want* her welcome if she comes ; we find,
 Riches to be but burthens to the mind.

Again.

WHO with a little cannot be content,
 Endures an everlasting punishment.

The Covetous still Captives.

LET'S live with that smal pittance that we have ;
 Who covets more, is evermore a slave.

Lawes.

WHEN Lawes full power have to sway, we see
 Little or no part there of Tyrannie.

Of Love.

I LE get me hence,
 Because no fence,
Or Fort that I can make here ;
 But Love by charmes,
 Or else by Armes
Will storme, or starving take here.

Upon Cock.

COCK calls his Wife his Hen : when *Cock* goes too't,
Cock treads his Hen, but treads her under-foot.

To his Muse.

GO wooe young *Charles* no more to looke,
    Then but to read this in my Booke :   [*than*
How *Herrick* beggs, if that he can-
Not like the Muse; to love the man,
Who by the Shepheards, sung (long since)
The Starre-led-birth of Charles the *Prince.*[7]

The bad season makes the Poet sad.

DULL to my selfe, and almost dead to these
    My many fresh and fragrant Mistresses :
Lost to all Musick now ; since every thing
Puts on the semblance here of sorrowing.
Sick is the Land to'th' heart ; and doth endure
More dangerous faintings by her desp'rate cure.
But if that golden Age wo'd come again,
And *Charles* here Rule, as he before did Raign ;
If smooth and unperplext the Seasons were,
As when the *Sweet Maria* livèd here :[8]

---

[7] See Memorial-Introduction on this and the rest.
[8] Q. Henrietta Maria, called Mary by Charles.

I sho'd delight to have my Curles halfe drown'd
In *Tyrian Dewes*, and Head with Roses crown'd.
And once more yet (ere I am laid out dead)
Knock at a Starre with my exalted Head.[9]

To Vulcan.

THY sooty *Godhead*, I desire
　　Still to be ready with thy fire :
That sho'd my Booke despisèd be,
Acceptance it might find of thee.

Like Pattern, like People.

THIS *is the height of Justice, that to doe*
　　Thy selfe, which thou put'st other men unto.
As great men lead ; the meaner follow on,
Or to the good, or evill action.

Purposes.

NO wrath of Men, or rage of Seas
　　Can shake a just mans purposes :
No threats of Tyrants, or the Grim
Visage of them can alter him ;
But what he doth at first entend,[1]
That he holds firmly to the end.

---

[9] Horace : Ode i. 1.　　　　[1] = purpose or stretch to.

To the Maids to walke abroad.

COME sit we under yonder Tree,
   Where merry as the Maids we'l be.
And as on *Primroses* we sit,
We'l venter [2] (if we can) at wit:
If not, at *Draw-gloves* [3] we will play;
So spend some minutes of the day:
Or else spin out the thread of sands,
Playing at *Questions* and *Commands:*
Or tell what strange Tricks Love can do,
By quickly making one of two.
Thus we will sit and talke; but tell
No cruell truths of *Philomell,*
Or *Phillis,* whom hard Fate forc't on,
To kill her selfe for *Demophon.*[4]
But Fables we'l relate; how *Jove*
Put on all shapes to get a Love:
As now a *Satyr,* then a *Swan;*
A *Bull* but then; and now a man.
Next we will act, how young men wooe;
And sigh, and kiss, as Lovers do:

[2] = venture. [3] A now unknown game. Halliwell's description
s. v. must be wrong. [4] Phillis = Phyllis, d. of the Thracian
king Sithon. Demophon, to whom she was betrothed, remaining
over-long absent in Attica, Phyllis, regarding herself as forgotten,
put an end to her life. (Ovid. Ar. Am. iii. 38).

And talke of Brides ; & who shall make
That wedding -smock, this Bridal-Cake ;
That Dress, this Sprig, that Leaf, this Vine ;
That smooth and silken Columbine.[5]
This done, we'l draw lots, who shall buy
And guild the Baies and Rosemary :
What Posies for our Wedding Rings ;
What gloves we'l give, and Ribanings :
And smiling at our selves, decree,
Who then the joyning *Priest* shall be.
What short sweet Prayers shall be said ;
And how the Posset shall be made
With Cream of Lillies (not of Kine)
And *Maiden's-blush*, for spicèd wine.
Thus, having talkt, we'l next commend
A kiss to each ; and *so we'l end.*

His own Epitaph.

AS wearied *Pilgrims*, once possest
    Of long'd-for lodging, go to rest :
So I, now having rid my way ;
Fix here my Button'd [6] Staffe and stay.
Youth (I confess) hath me mis-led ;
But Age hath brought me right to Bed.

---

[5] =a flower so named, like others in this poem.
[6] See Glossarial Index s. v.

A Nuptiall Verse to Mistresse Elizabeth Lee,
now Lady Tracie.[7]

SPRING with the Larke, most comely Bride, and
    meet
Your eager Bridegroome with *auspitious* feet.
The Morn's farre spent; and the immortaïl Sunne
Corrols [8] his cheeke, to see those Rites not done.
Fie, Lovely maid! Indeed you are too slow,
When to the Temple Love sho'd runne, not go.
Dispatch your dressing then; and quickly wed:
Then feast, and coy't a little; then to bed.
This day is Loves day; and this busie night
Is yours, in which you challeng'd are to fight
With such an arm'd, but such an easie Foe,
As will if you yeeld, lye down conquer'd too.
The Field is pitch't; but such must be your warres,
As that your kisses must out-vie the Starres.
Fall down together vanquisht both, and lye
Drown'd in the bloud of Rubies there, not die.

The Night-piece, to Julia.

1. HER Eyes the Glow-worme lend thee,
    The Shooting Starres attend thee;

[7] Elizabeth Leigh, d. of Thomas, 1st Lord Leigh of Stoneleigh, co. Warwick, married John, 3rd Viscount Tracy. She died in 1688: he in 1686.   [8] = corals, i. e. reddens like coral.

And the Elves also,
Whose little eyes glow,
Like the sparks of fire, befriend thee.

2. No *Will-o'th'-Wispe* mis-light thee ;
Nor Snake, or Slow-worme bite thee :
But on, on thy way
Not making a stay,
Since Ghost ther's none to affright thee.

3. Let not the darke thee cumber ;
What though the Moon do's slumber?
The Starres of the night
Will lend thee their light,
Like Tapers cleare without number.

4. Then *Julia* let me wooe thee,
Thus, thus to come unto me :
And when I shall meet
Thy silv'ry feet,
My soule I'le poure into thee.

To Sir Clipseby Crew.[9]

1. GIVE me wine, and give me meate,
To create in me a heate,
That my pulses high may beate.

[9] See former notes on Crewe.

2. Cold and hunger never yet
   Co'd a noble Verse beget;
   But your Boules with Sack repleat.

3. Give me these (my Knight) and try
   In a Minutes space how I
   Can runne mad, and Prophesie.

4. Then if any Peece proves new,
   And rare, Ile say (my dearest *Crew*)
   It was full enspir'd by you.

Good Luck not lasting.

I F well the Dice runne, lets applaud the cast :
   The happy fortune will not alwayes last.

A Kisse.

W HAT is a Kisse? Why this, as some approve ;
   The sure sweet-Sement,[1] Glue, and Lime of Love.

Glorie.

I MAKE no haste to have my Numbers read :
   Seldome comes Glorie till a man be dead.

---

[1] = cement.

Poets.

WANTONS we are ; and though our words be
    such,
Our Lives do differ from our Lines by much.

No despight to the dead.

REPROACH we may the living ; not the dead :
  'Tis cowardice to bite the buried.

To his Verses.

WHAT will ye (my poor Orphans) do
      When I must leave the World (and you)
Who'l give ye then a sheltring shed,
Or credit ye, when I am dead ?
Who'l let ye by their fire sit ?
Although ye have a stock of wit,
Already coin'd to pay for it.
I cannot tell ; unlesse there be
Some Race of old humanitie
Left (of the large heart, and long hand)
Alive, as Noble *Westmorland ;* [2]
Or gallant *Newark ;* [3] which brave two
May fost'ring fathers be to you.
If not ; expect to be no less
Ill us'd, then Babes left fatherless.   [*than*

---

[2] See former note and Memorial-Introduction.   [3] *Ibid.*

His Charge to Julia *at his Death.*

DEAREST of thousands, now the time drawes
    neere,
That with my Lines, my Life must full-stop here.
Cut off thy haires ; and let thy Teares be shed
Over my Turfe, when I am buried.
Then for *effusions*,[4] let none wanting be,
Or other Rites that doe belong to me ;
As Love shall helpe thee, when thou do'st go hence
Unto thy everlasting residence.

Upon Love.

IN a Dreame, Love bad me go
    To the Gallies there to Rowe ;
  In the Vision, I askt why ?
  Love, as briefly did reply;
'Twas better there to toyle, then prove   [*than*
The turmoiles they endure that love.
  I awoke, and then I knew
  What Love said was too too true :
  Henceforth therefore I will be
  As from Love, from trouble free.
None pities him that's in the snare,
And warn'd before, wo'd not beware.

    [4] See Glossarial Index s. v.

The Coblers Catch.

COME sit we by the fires side ;
    And roundly drinke we here ;
Till that we see our cheekes Ale-dy'd
And noses tann'd with Beere.

Upon Bran.   *Epig.*

WHAT made that mirth last night ? the neighbours
        say,
That *Bran* the Baker did his Breech bewray :
I rather thinke (though they may speake the worst)
'Twas to his Batch, but Leaven laid there first.

Upon Snare, *an Usurer.*

SNARE, ten i' th' hundred calls his wife ; and why ?
    Shee brings in much, by carnall usury.
He by extortion brings in three times more :
Say, who's the worst, th' exactor, or the whore ?

Upon Grudgings.

GRUDGINGS turnes bread to stones, when to
        the Poore
He gives an almes, and chides them from his doore.

Connubii Flores, or the well-wishes at Weddings.
Chorus Sacerdotum.

1. FROM the Temple to your home
   May a thousand blessings come !
And a sweet concurring stream
Of all joyes, to joyn with them.

Chorus Juvenum.

2.   Happy day
      Make no long stay
          Here
      In thy Sphere;
But give thy place to-night,
        That she,
        As Thee,
        May be
Partaker of this sight.
And since it was thy care
To see the Younglings wed ;
'Tis fit that Night, the Paire,
Sho'd see safe brought to Bed.

Chorus Senum.

3. Go to your banquet then, but use delight,
So as to rise still with an appetite.
Love is a thing most nice ; and must be fed
To such a height ; but never surfeited.

What is beyond the mean is ever ill :
'Tis best to feed Love ; but not over-fill:
Go then discreetly to the Bed of pleasure ;
And this remember, *Vertue keepes the measure.*

Chorus Virginum.

4. Luckie signes we have discri'd
   To encourage on the Bride ;
   And to these we have espi'd,
   Not a kissing *Cupid* flyes
   Here about, but has his eyes,
   To imply your Love is wise.

Chorus Pastorum.

5. Here we present a fleece
   To make a peece
   Of cloth ;
   Nor, Faire, must you be loth
   Your Finger to apply
   To huswiferie.
   Then, then begin
   To spin :
   And (Sweetling) marke you, what a Web will come
   Into your Chests, drawn by your painfull Thumb.[5]

---

[5] See Glossarial Index s. v.   The thumb was much employed in spinning : painfull = painstaking.

Chorus Matronarum.

6. Set you to your Wheele, and wax
   Rich, by the Ductile[6] Wool and Flax.
Yarne is an Income ;[7] and the Huswives thread
The Larder fils with meat ; the Bin with bread.

Chorus Senum.

7. Let wealth come in by comely thrift,
   And not by any sordid shift :
                'Tis haste
                Makes waste :
            Extreames have still their fault ;
The softest Fire makes the sweetest Mault.
Who gripes too hard the dry and slip'rie sand,
Holds none at all, or little in his hand.

Chorus Virginum.

8. Goddesse of Pleasure, Youth, and Peace,
   Give them the blessing of encrease :
   And thou *Lucina*, that do'st heare
   The vowes of those, that children beare :
   Whenas her Aprill houre drawes neare,
   Be thou then propitious there.

Chorus Juvenum.

Farre hence be all speech, that may anger move :
Sweet words must nourish soft and gentle Love.

⁼pliant, drawn out.   7 ⁼being made and sold.

Chorus omnium.

10. Live in the Love of Doves, and having told
　The Ravens [8] yeares, go hence more Ripe then old.

　　　　　　　　　　　　　　　　　　　　　[*than*

To his lovely Mistresses.

ONE night i' th' yeare, my dearest Beauties, come
　And bring those *dew-drink-offerings* to my
　　Tomb.
When thence ye see my reverend Ghost to rise,
And there to lick th' effusèd sacrifice :
Though palenes be the Livery that I weare,
Looke ye not wan, or colourlesse for feare.
Trust me, I will not hurt ye ; or once shew
The least grim looke, or cast a frown on you :
Nor shall the Tapers when I'm there, burn blew.
This I may do (perhaps) as I glide by,
Cast on my Girles a glance, and loving eye :
Or fold mine armes and sigh, because I've lost
The world so soon, and in it, you the most.
Then these, no feares more on your Fancies fall, [*than*
Though then I smile, and speake no words at all.

Upon Love.

A CHRISTALL Violl *Cupid* brought,
　Which had a juice in it :

　　[8] Supposed to live for centuries.

Of which who drank, he said no thought
    Of Love he sho'd admit.

2. I greedy of the prize, did drinke,
    And emptied soon the glasse ;
Which burnt me so, that I do thinke
    The fire of hell it was.

3. Give me my earthen Cups again,
    The Christall I contemne ;
Which, though enchas'd with Pearls, contain
    A deadly draught in them.

4. And thou, O *Cupid /* come not to
    My Threshold, since I see,
For all I have, or else can do,
    Thou still wilt cozen me.

Upon Gander. *Epig.*

SINCE *Gander* did his prettie Youngling [9] wed ;
    Gander (they say) doth each night pisse a-Bed :
What is the cause ?   Why *Gander* will reply,
    No Goose layes good eggs that is trodden drye.

Upon Lungs. *Epig.*

LUNGS (as some say) ne'r sets him down to eate,
    But that his breath do's Fly-blow all the meate.

[9] = young person or young one.   See Glossarial Index s. v.

The Beggar to Mab, *the* Fairie Queen.

PLEASE your Grace, from out your Store,
   Give an Almes to one that's poore,
That your mickle,[1] may have more.
Black I'm grown for want of meat ;
Give me then an Ant to eate ;
Or the cleft eare of a Mouse
Over-sowr'd in drinke of Souce : [2]
Or, *sweet Lady,* reach to me
The *Abdomen* of a Bee ;
Or commend a *Crickets-hip,*
Or his *Huckson,*[3] to my Scrip.
Give for bread, a little bit
Of a Pease,[4] that 'gins to chit,[5]
And my full thanks take for it.
Floure of Fuz-balls, that's too good[6]
For a man in needy-hood :
But the Meal of Mill-dust can
Well content a craving man.
Any Orts [7] the Elves refuse
Well will serve the Beggars use.
But if this may seem too much
For an Almes ; then give me such

---

[1] = much.　　　　　　　[2] = pickles.
[3] = huckle-bone, hip-bone.　　[4] An old singular : Paradise Lost
'pisum.'　　[5] = shoot.　　[6] See Glossarial Index s. v.　　[7] = scraps.

Little bits, that nestle there
In the Pris'ners *Panier.*[8]
So a blessing light upon
You, and mighty *Oberon :*
That your plenty last till when,
I return your Almes agen.

An end decreed.

LET'S be jocund while we may ;
   All things have an ending day :
And when once the Work is done ;
Fates revolve no Flax th'ave spun.

Upon a child.

HERE a pretty Baby lies
   Sung asleep with Lullabies :
Pray be silent, and not stirre
Th' easie earth that covers her.

Painting sometimes permitted.

IF Nature do deny
   Colours, let Art supply.

Farewell Frost, or welcome the Spring.

FLED are the Frosts, and now the Fields appeare
Re-cloth'd in fresh and verdant Diaper.[9]

---

[8] = pannier—single ' n ' in French.   [9] flower-wrought linen cloth.

Thaw'd are the snowes, and now the lusty Spring
Gives to each Mead a neat [1] enameling.
The Palms put forth their Gemmes,[2] and every Tree
Now swaggers in her Leavy gallantry.
The while the *Daulian Minstrell* [3] sweetly sings
With warbling Notes, her *Tyrrean* [4] sufferings.
What gentle Winds perspire ?   As if here
Never had been the *Northern Plunderer*
To strip the Trees, and Fields, to their distresse,
Leaving them to a pittied nakednesse.
And look how when a frantick Storme doth tear
A stubborn Oake, or Holme [5] (long growing there)
But lul'd to calmnesse, then succeeds a breeze
That scarcely stirs the nodding leaves of Trees :
So when this War (which tempest-like doth spoil)
Our salt, our Corn, our Honie, Wine, and Oile)
Falls to a temper, and doth mildly cast
His inconsiderate Frenzie off (at last)
The gentle Dove may, when these turmoils cease,
Bring in her Bill, once more, the *Branch of Peace.*

---

[1] = elegant.   [2] " A million emeralds break from the newly-
budded lime." *Maud.*   [3] = nightingale.   [4] = Terean.

[5] Holly, which is abundant in Devon, is called the Holme or
Hulves tree, but there is also the Holme-oak, and the context shows
it is meant here.

The Hag.

1. THE Hag is astride,
  This night for to ride ;
The Devill and shee together :
  Through thick, and through thin,
  Now out, and then in,
Though ne'r so foule be the weather.

2. A Thorn or a Burr [6]
  She takes for a Spurre :
With a lash of a Bramble she rides now,
  Through Brakes and through Bryars,
  O're Ditches, and Mires,
She followes the Spirit that guides now.

3. No Beast, for his food,
  Dares now range the wood ;
But husht in his laire he lies lurking :
  While mischeifs, by these,
  On Land and on Seas,
At noone of Night are a-working.

4. The storme will arise,
  And trouble the skies ;

[6] = burdock.

This night, and more for the wonder,
        The ghost from the Tomb
        Affrighted shall come,
Cal'd out by the clap of the Thunder.

Upon an old man a Residenciarie.[7]

TREAD Sirs, as lightly as ye can
        Upon the grave of this old man.
Twice fortie (bating but one year,
And thrice three weekes) he livèd here.
Whom gentle fate translated hence
To a more happy Residence.
Yet, Reader, let me tell thee this
(Which from his ghost a promise is)
If here ye will some few teares shed,
He'l never haunt ye now he's dead.

Upon Teares.

TEARES, though th'are here below the sinners
        brine,
Above they are the Angels spicèd wine.

---

[7] = one who has been " in residence," i. e. living in the one parish
all his life-long.   In this town of Blackburn I know an old man
(upwards of 80) who has never been seven miles from his native home
here.

Physitians.

PHYSITIANS fight not against men ; but these
Combate for men, by conquering the disease.

The Primitiæ *to Parents.*

OUR *Houshold-gods* our Parents be ;
    And manners good requires, that we
The first-Fruits give to them, who gave
Us hands to get what here we have.

Upon Cob. *Epig.*

COB clouts his shooes, and as the story tells,
    His thumb-nailes-par'd, afford him sperrables.[8]

Upon Lucie. *Epig.*

SOUND Teeth has *Lucie,* pure as Pearl, and small,
    With mellow Lips, and luscious there withall.

Upon Skoles. *Epig.*

SKOLES stinks so deadly, that his Breeches loath
    His dampish Buttocks furthermore to cloath :
Cloy'd they are up with Arse ; but hope, one blast
Will whirle about, and blow them thence at last.

[8] = small nails.

To Silvia.

I AM holy, while I stand
    Circum-crost [9] by thy pure hand :
But when that is gone ; Again,
I, as others, am *Prophane.*

To his Closet-Gods.

WHEN I goe Hence, ye *Closet-Gods*, I feare
    Never againe to have ingression [1] here :
Where I have had, what ever things co'd be
Pleasant, and precious to my Muse and me.
Besides rare sweets, I had a Book which none
Co'd reade the Intext [2] but my selfe alone.
About the Cover of this Book there went
A curious-comely clean *Compartlement* :[3]
And, in the midst, to grace it more, was set
A blushing-pretty-peeping Rubelet :[4]
But now 'tis clos'd ; and being shut, & seal'd,
Be it, O be it, never more reveal'd !
Keep here still, *Closet-Gods*, 'fore whom I've set
Oblations oft, of sweetest Marmelet.[5]

---

[9] = her hand around his, grasping it lover-like.
[1] = entrance.   [2] = the text (within).
[3] diminutive of ' compartment,' which meant a border in gardening, or the ornamental bordering around maps, pictures, &c., or as here, the corner of a book.   [4] *Ibid* of ' ruby.'   [5] = märmalade.

A Bacchanalian Verse.

1. FILL me a mighty Bowle
    Up to the brim :
    That I may drink
Unto my *Johnsons* soule.

2. Crowne it agen agen ;
    And thrice repeat
    That happy heat ;
    To drink to Thee my *Ben.*

3. Well I can quaffe, I see,
    To th' number five,
    Or nine ; but thrive
In frenzie ne'r like thee.

Long lookt for comes at last.

THOUGH long it be, yeeres may repay the debt ;
None loseth that, which he in time may get.

To Youth.

DRINK Wine, and live here blithefull, while ye
    may :
The morrowes life too late is, Live to-day.

Never too late to dye.

NO man comes late unto that place from whence
    Never man yet had a regredience.[6]

A Hymne to the Muses.

O ! YOU the Virgins nine !
    That doe our soules encline
To noble Discipline !
Nod to this vow of mine :
Come then, and now enspire
My violl and my lyre
With your eternall fire :
And make me one entire
Composer in your Quire.
Then I'le your Altars strew
With Roses sweet and new ;
And ever live a true
Acknowledger of you.

On himselfe.

ILE sing no more, nor will I longer write
    Of that sweet Lady, or that gallant Knight :
Ile sing no more of Frosts, Snowes, Dews and Showers ;
No more of Groves, Meades, Springs, and wreaths of
        Flowers :

[6] = return : " from whose bourne no traveller returns." Hamlet
iii. 1.

Ile write no more, nor will I tell or sing
Of *Cupid*, and his wittie coozning :[7]
Ile sing no more of death, or shall the grave
No more my Dirges, and my Trentalls [8] have.

Upon Jone *and* Jane.

J ONE is a wench that's painted ;
Jone is a Girle that's tainted ;
Yet *Jone* she goes
Like one of those
Whom purity had Sainted.

Jane is a Girle that's prittie ;
Jane is a wench that's wittie ;
Yet, who wo'd think,
Her breath do's stinke,
As so it doth ? that's pittie.

To Momus.

W HO read'st this Book that I have writ,
And can'st not mend, but carpe at it :
By all the muses ! thou shalt be
Anathema to it, and me.

Ambition.

I N wayes to greatnesse, think on this,
That slippery all Ambition is.

---

[7] = cozening.   [8] See Glossarial Index s. v.

The Country life, to the honoured M. End. Porter,
  Groome of the Bed-Chamber to His Maj.[9]

S̲WEET Country life, to such unknown,
  Whose lives are others, not their own !
But serving Courts, and Cities, be '
Less happy, less enjoying thee.
Thou never Plow'st the Oceans foame
To seek, and bring rough Pepper home :
Nor to the Eastern Ind dost rove
To bring from thence the scorchèd Clove.
Nor, with the losse of thy lov'd rest,
Bring'st home the Ingot [1] from the West.
No, thy Ambition's Master-piece
Flies no thought higher then a fleece :   [*than*
Or how to pay thy Hinds, and cleere
All scores ; and so to end the yeere :
But walk'st about thine own dear bounds,
Not envying others larger grounds :
For well thou know'st, *'tis not th' extent*
Of Land makes life, but sweet content.
When now the Cock (the Plow-mans Horne)
Calls forth the lilly-wristed [2] Morne ;

---

[9] See former note.   [1] = uncoined gold.
  " Nereids lily-wristed."   Sorrows of Hyperion.

Then to thy corn-fields thou dost goe,
Which though well soyl'd,[3] yet thou dost know,
That the best compost for the Lands
Is the wise Masters Feet, and Hands.
There at the Plough thou find'st thy Teame,
With a Hind whistling there to them :
And cheer'st them up, by singing how
The Kingdoms portion is *the Plow*.
This done, then to th' enameld Meads
Thou go'st, and as thy foot there treads,
Thou seest a present God-like Power
Imprinted in each Herbe and Flower :
And smell'st the breath of great-ey'd Kine,
Sweet as the blossomes of the Vine.
Here thou behold'st thy large sleek Neat [4]
Unto the Dew-laps[5] up in meat :
And, as thou look'st, the wanton Steere,
The Heifer, Cow, and Oxe draw neere
To make a pleasing pastime there.
These seen, thou go'st to view thy flocks
Of sheep, (safe from, the Wolfe and Fox)
And find'st their bellies there as full
Of short sweet grasse, as backs with wool.

[3] = manured.   [4] = cattle, oxen, cows, &c.
[5] = loose skin on throat of kine.

And leav'st them (as they feed and fill)
A Shepherd piping on a hill.
For Sports, for Pagentrie, and Playes,
Thou hast thy Eves, and Holydayes:
On which the young men and maids meet,
To exercise their dancing feet:
Tripping the comely country Round,[6]
With Daffadils and Daisies crown'd.
Thy Wakes, thy Quintels,[7] here thou hast,
Thy May-poles too with Garlands grac't:
Thy Morris-dance; thy Whitsun-ale;
Thy Sheering[8]-feast, which never faile.
Thy Harvest home; thy Wassaile bowle,
That's tost up after Fox i' th' Hole.[9]
Thy Mummeries;[10] thy Twelfe-tide Kings
And Queenes; thy Christmas revellings:
Thy Nut-browne mirth; thy Russet wit;
And no man payes too deare for it.
To these, thou hast thy times to goe
And trace the Hare i' th' trecherous Snow:
Thy witty wiles to draw, and get
The Larke into the Trammell net :[1]

[6] See Glossarial Index s. v.   [7] Ibid.
[8] = Harvest-feast.   [9] See Glossarial Index s. v.
[10] masqueradings or maskings.   [1] = a net for birds and for fish.

Thou hast thy Cockrood,[2] and thy Glade[3]
To take the precious Phesant made :
Thy Lime-twigs, Snares, and Pit-falls then
To catch the pilfring Birds, not Men.
O happy life ! if that their good
The Husbandmen but understood !
Who all the day themselves doe please,
And Younglings, with such sports as these.
And, lying down, have nought t' affright
Sweet sleep, that makes more short the night.

Cætera desunt ————   .

To Electra.

1. I DARE not ask a kisse ;
      I dare not beg a smile ;
    Lest having that, or this,
      I might grow proud the while.

2. No, no, the utmost share
      Of my desire, shall be
    Onely to kisse that Aire,
      That lately kissèd thee.

[2] road or walk.
[3] open space in a wood made for snaring pheasants, &c.

To his worthy friend, M. Arthur Bartly.[4]

WHEN after many Lusters[5] thou shalt be
 Wrapt up in Seare-cloth with thine Ancestrie :
When of thy ragg'd *Escutcheons* shall be seene
So little left, as if they ne'r had been :
Thou shalt thy Name have, and thy Fames best trust,
Here with the Generation of my Just.

What kind of Mistresse he would have.

BE the Mistresse of my choice,
 Cleane in manners, cleere in voice :
Be she witty, more then wise ;   [*than*
Pure enough, though not Precise :
Be she shewing in her dresse,
Like a civill [6] Wilderness ;
That the curious may detect
Order in a sweet neglect :
Be she rowling in her eye,
Tempting all the passers by :
And each Ringlet of her haire,
An Enchantment, or a Snare,
For to catch the Lookers on ;
But her self held fast by none.

----

[4] Unknown.   [5] See Glossarial Index s. v.   [6] *Ibid.*

Let her *Lucrece* all day be,
Thais in the night, to me.
Be she such, as neither will
Famish me, nor over-fill.

Upon Zelot.

IS *Zelot* pure? he is : ye see he weares
The signe of *Circumcision*[7] in his eares.

The Rosemarie branch.

GROW for two ends, it matters not at all,
Be't for my *Bridall*, or my *Buriall*.[8]

Upon Madam Ursly. *Epig.*

FOR ropes of pearle,[9] first Madam *Vrsly* showes
A chaine of Cornes, pickt from her eares and
toes :
Then, next, to match *Tradescant's*[1] curious shels,
Nailes from her fingers mew'd, she shewes : what els ?
Why then (forsooth) a Carcanet[2] is shown
Of teeth, as deaf as nuts,[3] and all her own.

---

[7] = a wicked reference to cropping of the ears.   [8] Rosemary
being used at both.   [9] = 'chains of pearle,' as in Donne.
[1] An early naturalist whose collection is in the Ashmolean Mu-
seum at Oxford.   [2] See Glossarial Index s. v.
[3] It is difficult to explain the supposed deafness of nuts.

Upon Crab. *Epig.*

CRAB faces gownes with sundry Furres ; 'tis
    known,
He keeps the Fox-furre for to face his own.

A Paranæticall, or Advisive Verse, to his
friend, M. John Wicks.[4]

IS this a life, to break thy sleep ?
    To rise as soon as day doth peep ?
To tire thy patient Oxe or Asse
By noone, and let thy good dayes passe,
Not knowing This, that *Jove* decrees
Some mirth, t'adulce[5] mans miseries ?
No ; 'tis a life, to have thine oyle,
Without extortion, from thy soyle :
Thy faithfull fields to yeeld thee Graine,
Although with some, yet little paine :
To have thy mind, and nuptiall bed,
With feares, and cares uncumberèd :
A pleasing Wife, that by thy side
Lies softly panting like a Bride.
This is to live, and to endeere
Those minutes, Time has lent us here.

---

⁴ See Memorial-Introduction.   ⁵ = sweeten.

Then, while Fates suffer, live thou free,
(As is that ayre that circles thee)
And crown thy temples too, and let
Thy servant, not thy own self, sweat,
To strut[7] thy barnes with sheafs of Wheat.
Time steals away like to a stream,
And we glide hence away with them.
No sound recalls the houres once fled,
Or Roses, being witherèd :
Nor us (my Friend) when we are lost,
Like to a Deaw, or melted Frost.
Then live we mirthfull, while we should,
And turn the iron Age to Gold.
Let's feast, and frolick, sing, and play,
And thus lesse last, then live our Day.   [*than*
Whose life with care is overcast,
That man's not said to live, but last :
Nor is't a life, seven yeares to tell,
But for to live that half seven well :
And that wee'l do ; as men, who know,
Some few sands spent, we hence must go,
Both to be blended in the Urn,
From whence there's never a return.

---

[7] = swell : see Glossarial Index s. v.

Once seen, and no more.

THOUSANDS each day passe by, which wee,
  Once past and gone, no more shall see.

Love.

THIS Axiom I have often heard,
  Kings ought to be more lov'd, then fear'd.   [*than*

To M. Denham, *on his Prospective Poem.*[8]

OR lookt I back unto the Times hence flown
    To praise those Muses, and dislike our own ?
Or did I walk those *Pean*-Gardens[9] through,
To kick the Flow'rs, and scorn their odours too ?
I might (and justly) be reputed (here)
One nicely mad, or peevishly severe.
But by *Apollo !* as I worship wit,
(Where I have cause to burn perfumes to it :)
So, I confesse, 'tis somwhat to do well
In our high art, although we can't excell,
Like thee ; or dare the Buskins to unloose
Of thy brave, bold, and sweet *Maronian* Muse.[1]

---

[8] Sir John Denham and his " Cooper Hill : " originally published
in 1642.

[9] In heraldry pean is when the field or ground is of sable and the
powderings *or.* ·   [1] ' Maronian ' i. e. Virgilian.

But since I'm cal'd (rare *Denham*) to be gone,
Take from thy *Herrick* this conclusion :
'Tis dignity in others, if they be
Crown'd Poets ; yet live Princes under thee :
The while their wreaths and Purple Robes do shine,
Lesse by their own jemms, then those beams of
        thine.   [*than*

A Hymne, to the Lares.[2]

IT was, and still my care is,
   To worship ye, the *Lares*,
With crowns of greenest Parsley,
And Garlick chives[3] not scarcely :
For favours here to warme me,
And not by fire to harme me.
For gladding so my hearth here,
With inoffensive mirth here ;
That while the Wassaile Bowle here
With *North-down* Ale doth troule[4] here,
No sillable doth fall here,
To marre the mirth at all here.
For which, ô *Chimney-keepers !*
(I dare not call ye Sweepers)

---

[2] See Glossarial Index s. v.   [3] *Ibid.*   [4] = pass about.

So long as I am able
To keep a countrey-table,
Great be my fare, or small cheere,
I'le eat and drink up all here.

Deniall in women no disheartning to men.

WOMEN, although they ne're so goodly make it,
  Their fashion is, but to say no, to take it.

Adversity.

LOVE is maintain'd by wealth ; when all is spent,
  Adversity then breeds the discontent.

To Fortune.

TUMBLE me down, and I will sit
    Upon my ruines (smiling yet :) [5]
Teare me to tatters ; yet I'le be
Patient in my necessitie.
Laugh at my scraps of cloaths, and shun
Me, as a fear'd infection :
Yet scarre-crow-like I'le walk, as one,
Neglecting thy derision.

[5] Pronounced ' yit ' in Suffolk still.

To Anthea.

COME, *Anthea*, know thou this,
   Love at no time idle is :
Let's be doing, though we play
But at push-pin[6] (half the day :)
Chains of sweet bents[7] let us make,
Captive one, or both, to take :
In which bondage we will lie,
Soules transfusing thus, and die.

Cruelties.

NERO commanded ; but withdrew his eyes
   From the beholding Death, and cruelties.

Perseverance.

HAST thou begun an act ? ne're then give o're :
   No man despaires to do what's done before.

Upon his Verses.

WHAT off-spring other men have got,
   The how, where, when, I question not.
These are the Children I have left;
Adopted some ; none got by theft.
But all are toucht [8] (like lawfull plate)
And no Verse illegitimate.

[6] See Glossarial Index s. v.   [7] = a coarse moor grass.
[8] stamped as at Goldsmiths' Hall.

Distance betters Dignities.

K INGS must not oft be seen by publike eyes ;
  State at a distance adds to dignities.

Health.

H EALTH is no other (as the learnèd hold)
  But a just measure both of Heat and Cold.

To Dianeme.   *A Ceremonie in Glocester.*

I LE to thee a Simnell? bring,
  'Gainst thou go'st a *mothering ;* [10]
So that, when she blesseth thee,
Half that blessing thou'lt give me.

To the King.

G IVE way, give way, now, now my *Charles* shines
      here,
A Publike Light (in this immensive Sphere,)
Some starres were fixt before ; but these are dim,
Compar'd (in this my ample Orbe) to Him.
Draw in your feeble fiers, while that He
Appeares but in His Meaner Majestie.

[9] A kind of cake of fine flour made for Midlent or Mothering
Sunday, when children grown and in the world visited their parents
and presented them with cakes, &c.   [10] See last note.

Where, if such glory flashes from His Name,
Which is His Shade, who can abide His Flame !
Princes, and such like Publike Lights as these,
Must not be lookt on, but at distances :
For, if we gaze on These brave Lamps too neer,
Our eyes they'l blind, or if not blind, they'l bleer.

The Funerall Rites of the Rose.

THE Rose was sick, and smiling di'd ;
      And (being to be sanctifi'd)
About the Bed, there sighing stood
The sweet, and flowrie Sisterhood.
Some hung the head, while some did bring
(To wash her) water from the Spring.
Some laid her forth, while others wept,
But all a solemne Fast there kept.
The holy Sisters some among
The sacred *Dirge* and *Trentall*[1] sung.
But ah ! what sweets smelt every where,
As Heaven had spent all perfumes there.
At last, when prayers for the dead,
And Rites were all accomplishèd ;
They, weeping, spread a Lawnie Loome,
And clos'd her up, as in a. Tombe.

[1] See Glossarial Index s. v.

The Rainbow : or, curious Covenant.

MINE eyes, like clouds, were drizling raine,
  And as they thus did entertaine
The gentle Beams from *Julia's* sight
To mine eyes level'd opposite :
O Thing admir'd ! there did appeare
A curious Rainbow smiling there ;
Which was the Covenant, that she
No more wo'd drown mine eyes, or me.

The last stroke strike sure.

THOUGH by well-warding many blowes w'ave
  past,
That stroke most fear'd is, which is struck the last.

Fortune.

FORTUNE'S a blind profuser of her own,
  Too much she gives to some, enough to none.

Stool-ball.

 1. AT Stool-ball,[2] *Lucia*, let us play,
   For Sugar-cakes and Wine ;

---

 [2] A play wherein balls were driven from stool to stool.

Or for a Tansie³ let us pay,
    The losse or thine, or mine.

2. If thou, my Deere, a winner be
    At trundling of the Ball,
The wager thou shalt have, and me,
    And my misfortunes all.

3. But if (my Sweetest) I shall get,
    Then I desire but this ;
That likewise I may pay the Bet,
    And have for all a kisse.

To Sappho.

LET us now take time, and play,
    Love, and live here while we may ;
Drink rich wine ; and make good cheere,
While we have our being here :
For, once dead, and laid i'th grave,
No return from thence we have.

On Poet Prat.   *Epig.*

PRAT he writes Satyres ; but herein's the fault,
    In no one Satyre there's a mite of salt.

---

³ = pan-cake, made of the plant, which was a common wager or
prize at the game.

Upon Tuck. Epig.

AT Post and Paire, or Slam, *Tom Tuck*[4] would
      play
This Christmas, but his want wherwith, sayes Nay.

Biting of Beggars.

WHO, railing, drives the Lazar from his door,
      Instead of almes, sets dogs upon the poor.

The May-pole.

THE May-pole is up,
      Now give me the cup ;
I'le drink to the Garlands a-round it :
      But first unto those
      Whose hands did compose
The glory of flowers that crown'd it.

A health to my Girles,
      Whose husbands may Earles
Or Lords be, (granting my wishes)
      And when that ye wed
      To the Bridall Bed,
Then multiply all, like to Fishes.

[4] = games at cards.

Men mind no state in sicknesse.

THAT flow of Gallants which approach
　　To kisse thy hand from out the coach ;
That fleet of Lackeyes, which do run
Before thy swift Postilion :
Those strong-hoof'd Mules, which we behold,
Rein'd in with Purple, Pearl, and gold,
And shod with silver, prove to be
The drawers of the *axeltree.*
Thy Wife, thy Children, and the state
Of *Persian* Loomes, and *antique* Plate :
All these, and more, shall then afford
No joy to thee their sickly Lord.

Adversity.

ADVERSITY hurts none, but onely such
　　Whom whitest Fortune dandled has too much.

Want.

NEED is no vice at all ; though here it be,
　　With men, a loathèd inconveniencie.

Griefe.

SORROWES divided amongst many, lesse
　　Discruciate [5] a man in deep distresse.

[5] = crucify, put to torture.

Love palpable.

I PREST my *Julia's* lips, and in the kisse
  Her Soule and Love were palpable in this.

No Action hard to affection.

NOTHING hard, or harsh can prove
  Unto those that truly love.

Meane things overcome mighty.

BY the weak'st means things mighty are o'rethrown.
  He's Lord of thy life, who contemnes his own.[6]

Upon Trigg.   *Epig.*

TRIGG having turn'd his sute, he struts in state,
  And tells the world, he's now regenerate.

Upon Smeaton.

HOW co'd *Luke Smeaton* weare a shoe, or boot,
  Who two and thirty cornes had on a foot.

The Bracelet of Pearle: to Silvia.

I BRAKE thy Bracelet 'gainst my will;
  And, wretched, I did see

[6] See Glossarial Index s. v.

Thee discomposèd then, and still
    Art discontent with me.

One jemme was lost ; and I will get
    A richer pearle for thee,
Then ever, dearest *Silvia*, yet   [*than*
    Was drunk to *Antonie*.[7]

Or, for revenge, I'le tell thee what
    Thou for the breach shalt do ;
First, crack the strings, and after that,
    Cleave thou my heart in two.

How Roses came red.

'TIS said, as *Cupid* danc't among
    The *Gods*, he down the Nectar flung ;
Which, on the white *Rose* being shed,
Made it for ever after red.

Kings.

MEN are not born Kings, but are men renown'd ;
    Chose first, confirm'd next, & at last are
    crown'd.

---

[7] Viz. by Cleopatra—a common-place of classical history.

First work, and then wages.

PREPOST'ROUS[8] is that order, when we run
 To ask our wages, e're our work be done.

Teares, and Laughter.

KNEW'ST thou, one moneth wo'd take thy life
  away,
Thou'dst weep ; but laugh, sho'd it not last a day.

Glory.

GLORY no other thing is (*Tullie* sayes)[9]
 Then a mans frequent Fame, spoke out with
   praise.   [*than*

Possessions.

THOSE possessions short-liv'd are,
 Into the which we come by warre.

Laxare fibulam.

TO loose the button, is no lesse,
 Then to cast off all bashfulnesse.[1]   [*than*

---

[8] = inverted.   [9] See Cicero *frequenter* s. v. *fama.*
[1] i. e. in gluttonous greed to take more and still more.

His returne to London.[2]

FROM the dull confines of the drooping West,
    To see the day spring from the pregnant East,
Ravisht in spirit, I come, nay more, I flie
To thee, blest place of my Nativitie !
Thus, thus with hallowed foot I touch the ground,
With thousand blessings by thy Fortune crown'd.
O fruitfull Genius ! that bestowest here
An everlasting plenty, yeere by yeere.
O *Place !* O *People !* Manners ! fram'd to please
All Nations, Customes, Kindreds, Languages !
I am a free-born *Roman ;* suffer then,
That I amongst you live a Citizen.
London my home is : though by hard fate sent
Into a long and irksome banishment ;
Yet since cal'd back ; henceforward let me be,
O native countrey, repossest by thee !
For, rather then I'le to the West return,   [*than*
I'le beg of thee first here to have mine Urn.
Weak I am grown, and must in short time fall ;
Give thou my sacred Reliques Buriall.

[2] See our Memorial-Introduction on this.

Not every day fit for Verse.

'TIS not ev'ry day, that I
    Fitted am to prophesie :
No, but when the Spirit fils
The fantastick Pannicles :[3]
Full of fier ; then I write
As the Godhead doth indite.
Thus inrag'd, my lines are hurl'd,
Like the *Sybells*,[4] through the world.
Look how next the holy fier
Either slakes, or doth retire ;
So the Fancie cooles, till when
That brave Spirit comes agen.

Poverty the greatest pack.[5]

TO mortall men great loads allotted be,
    But of all packs, no pack like poverty.

---

[3] Topsell ("Beasts," 1607, p. 308) observes of 'head-ache' that
"It commeth either of some inward causes, as of some cholerick
humour, bred in the *pannicles* of the braine, or else of some outward
cause : " = cells, i. e. the organs of the 'phantasy' or fancy.
[4] = Sybils.   [5] = load (as of the 'packman' or chap-man).

A Beucolick,[6] *or discourse of Neatherds.*[7]

1. COME blithefull Neatherds, let us lay
   A wager, who the best shall play,
   Of thee, or I, the Roundelay,
   That fits the businesse of the Day.

Chor. And *Lallage* the Judge shall be,
   To give the prize to thee, or me.

2. Content, begin, and I will bet
   A Heifer smooth, and black as jet,
   In every part alike compleat,
   And wanton as a Kid as yet.

Chor. And *Lallage* (with cow-like eyes)
   Shall be Disposeresse[8] of the prize.

1. Against thy Heifer, I will here
   Lay to thy stake a lustie Steere,
   With gilded hornes,[9] and burnisht cleere.

Chor. Why then begin, and let us heare
   The soft, the sweet, the mellow note
   That gently purles [1] from eithers Oat.[2]

---

[6] = bucolic or pastoral.   [7] = oxen or cattle herds.
[8] A coinage of Herrick's own, apparently.
[9] Juvenal s. v.   [1] See Glossarial Index s. v.   [2] *Ibid*

   2. The stakes are laid : let's now apply
      Each one to make his melody :

Lal. The equall Umpire shall be I,
     Who'l hear, and so judge righteously.

Chor. Much time is spent in prate ; begin,
      And sooner play, the sooner win.   [*He playes.*

   1. That's sweetly touch't, I must confesse :
      Thou art a man of worthinesse :
      But hark how I can now expresse
      My love unto my Neatherdesse.[3]   [*He sings.*

Chor. A suger'd[4] note ! and sound as sweet
      As Kine, when they at milking meet.

   1. Now for to win thy Heifer faire,
      I'le strike thee such a nimble Ayre,
      That thou shalt say (thy selfe) 'tis rare ;
      And title me [5] without compare.

Chor. Lay by a while your Pipes, and rest,
      Since both have here deservèd best.

---

[3] = shepherdess of cattle.

[4] From Sidney to Shakespeare and onward, a favourite word or phrase.

[5] = entitle me one beyond all comparison, a sweet player.

2. To get thy Steerling,[6] once again,
   I'le play thee such another strain;
   That thou shalt swear, my Pipe do's raigne
   Over thine Oat,[7] as Soveraigne. [*He sings.*

Chor. And *Lallage* shall tell by this,
   Whose now the prize and wager is.

1. Give me the prize: 2. The day is mine:
1. Not so; my Pipe has silenc't thine:
   And hadst thou wager'd twenty Kine,
   They were mine own. *Lal.* In love combine.

Chor. And lay we down our Pipes together,
   As wearie, not o'recome by either.[8]

True safety.[9]

'TIS not the Walls, or purple, that defends
   A Prince from Foes; but 'tis his Fort of Friends.

A Prognostick.

AS many Lawes and Lawyers do expresse
   Nought but a Kingdoms ill-affectednesse:

---

[6] = diminutive of ' steer,' an oxen of the 3rd year.
[7] See Glossarial Index s. v.
[8] Et vitulâ tu dignus, et hic. Virgil. Ecl. 3. N.
[9] See Sophocles ' Œdipus Tyrannus.'

Ev'n so, those streets and houses do but show
Store of diseases, where Physitians flow.

Upon Julia's *sweat.*

WO'D ye oyle of Blossomes get ?
   Take it from my *Julia's* sweat :
Oyl of Lillies, and of Spike,
From her moysture take the like :
Let her breath, or let her blow,
All rich spices thence will flow.

Proof to no purpose.

YOU see this gentle streame, that glides,
   Shov'd on, by quick-succeeding Tides :
Trie if this sober streame you can
Follow to th' wilder Ocean :
And see, if there it keeps unspent
In that congesting element.
Next, from that world of waters, then
By poares and cavernes back agen
Induc't that inadultrate same
Streame to the Spring from whence it came.
This with a wonder when ye do,
As easie, and els easier too :

[1] See Memorial-Introduction for parallel from Southwell.

Then may ye recollect [2] the graines
Of my particular Remaines ;
After a thousand Lusters hurld,
By ruffling winds, about the world.

Fame.

*'TIS still observ'd, that Fame ne're sings
The order, but the Sum of things.*

By use comes easinesse.

OFT bend the Bow, and thou with ease shalt do,
What others can't with all their strength put to.

To the Genius of his house.

COMMAND the Roofe, great *Genius*, and from
      thence
Into this house powre downe thy influence,
That through each room a golden pipe may run
Of living water by thy *Benizon*.[3]
Fulfill [4] the Larders, and with strengthning bread
Be evermore these Bynns replenishèd.
Next, like a Bishop consecrate my ground,
That luckie Fairies here may dance their Round :

[2] = re-gather.
[3] = blessing, benediction.   [4] = fill full.

And after that, lay downe some silver pence,
The Masters charge and care to recompence.
Charme then the chambers ; make the beds for ease,
More then for peevish pining sicknesses.   [*than*
Fix the foundation fast, and let the Roofe
Grow old with time, but yet keep weather-proofe.

His Grange,[5] *or private wealth.*

THOUGH Clock,
  To tell how night drawes hence, I've none,
    A Cock,
I have, to sing how day drawes on.
    I have
A maid (my *Prew*) by good luck sent,
    To save
That little, Fates me gave or lent.
    A Hen
I keep, which creeking [6] day by day,
    Tells when
She goes her long white egg to lay.
    A Goose
I have, which, with a jealous eare,

[5] = farm-house or a residence.
[6] = craking, creaking : imitative word, i. e. of the peculiar notes
emitted by the hen when it has laid an egg.

Lets loose

Her tongue, to tell what danger's neare.

A Lamb

I keep (tame) with my morsells fed,

Whose Dam

An Orphan left him (lately dead.)

A Cat

I keep, that playes about my House,

Grown fat,

With eating many a miching [7] Mouse.

To these

A *Trasy* [8] I do keep, whereby

I please

The more my rurall privacie :

Which are

But toyes, to give my heart some ease :

Where care

None is, slight things do lightly please.

---

[7] = thieving, with slyness, and creeping softly implied. In Devonshire still it means truant, and is pronounced mich : in Somerset, meich (the i as in sigh). It is a Shakesperean word, " marry this miching " (Hamlet iii. 2).

[8] His spaniel. H. So called probably from the ' tracing ' or following of game. See Glossarial Index s. v.

Good precepts, or counsell.

IN all thy need, be thou possest
 Still with a well-prepar**è**d brest :[9]
Nor let the shackles make thee sad ;
Thou canst but have, what others had.
And this for comfort thou must know,
Times that are ill wo'nt still be so.[1]
Clouds will not ever powre down raine ;
A sullen day will cleere againe.[2]
First, peales. of Thunder we must heare,
Then Lutes and Harpes shall stroke the eare.

Money makes the mirth.

WHEN all Birds els do of their musick faile,
 Money's the still-sweet-singing *Nightingale.*

Up tailes all.[3]

BEGIN with a kisse,
 Go on too with this :

---

[9] ....."bene præparatum pectus." Horace, Od. ii. 10. 14.
 [1] " Non, si male nunc, et olim
  Sic erit." Horace, Od. ii. 10. 17.
  [2] " Non semper imbres nubibus hispidos
   Manant in agros." Horat. Ode 9, Lib. 2. N.
[3] = riotous, clamorous confusion, but with a double meaning.

And thus, thus, thus let us smother.
 Our lips for a while,
 But let's not beguile
Our hope of one for the other.

 This play, be assur'd,
 Long enough has endur'd,
Since more and more is exacted ;
 For love he doth call
 For his Uptailes all ;
And that's the part to be acted.

Upon Franck.

FRANCK wo'd go scoure her teeth ; and setting
 to't
Twice two fell out, all rotten at the root.

Upon Lucia *dabled in the deaw.*

MY *Lucia* in the deaw did go,
 And prettily bedabled [4] so,
Her cloaths held up, she shew'd withall
 Her decent [5] legs, cleane, long and small.
 I follow'd after to descrie
 Part of the nak't sincerity ; [6]

---

[4] See Glossarial Index s. v.

[5] = beautiful.   Horace : Od. i. 18, 6, "teque, *decens* Venus." Cf. Od. iv. 1, 13, 1, 17.   [6] See Glossarial Index s. v. : so 'nak't *simplicities* ' (*Ibid*).

But still the envious Scene [7] between
Deni'd the Mask [8] I wo'd have seen.

Charon *and* Phylomel, *a Dialogue sung.*
Ph. CHARON *!* O gentle *Charon !* let me wooe
      thee,
By tears and pitie now to come unto mee.
Ch. What voice so sweet and charming do I heare?
Say what thou art. *Ph.* I prithee first draw
      neare.
Ch. A sound I heare, but nothing yet can see,
Speak where thou art. *Ph.* O *Charon* pittie me !
I am a bird, and though no name I tell,
My warbling note will say I'm *Phylomel.*
Ch. What's that to me, I waft nor fish or fowles,
Nor Beasts (fond [9] thing) but only humane soules.
Ph. Alas for me ! *Ch.* Shame on thy witching note,
That made me thus hoist saile, and bring my
      Boat :
But Ile returne ; what mischief brought thee
      hither?
Ph. A deale of Love, and much, much Griefe to-
      gether.

[7] i. e. the drop-scene (or ' scene ' in the classical sense).
[8] = play going on : hence anything between the scene, i. e. Lucia
herself in this place.   [9] = foolish.

Ch. What's thy request ?   *Ph.* That since she's now beneath
Who fed my life, I'le follow her in death.[1]
Ch. And is that all ? I'm gone.   *Ph.* By love I pray thee.
Ch. Talk not of love, all pray, but few soules pay me.
Ph. Ile give thee vows & tears.   *Ch.* Can tears pay skores
For mending sails, for patching Boat and Oares ?
Ph. I'le beg a penny, or Ile sing so long,
Till thou shalt say, I've paid thee with a song.
Ch. Why then begin, and all the while we make
Our slothfull passage o're the Stygian Lake,
Thou & I'le sing to make these dull Shades merry,
Who els with tears wo'd doubtles drown my ferry.

Upon Paul. *Epigr.*

PAULS hands do give ; what give they, bread or meat,
Or money? no, but onely deaw and sweat.
As stones and salt gloves [2] use to give, even so
Pauls hands do give, nought else for ought we know.

---

[1] Here Philomel is male.   [2] See Glossarial Index s. v.

Upon Sibb. *Epigr.*

SIBB when she saw her face how hard it was,
   For anger spat on thee her Looking-glasse :
But weep not, *Christall;* for the shame was meant
Not unto thee, but That thou didst present.

A Ternarie of littles, upon a pipkin of Jellie sent to a Lady.

1. A LITTLE Saint best fits a little Shrine,
   A little prop best fits a little Vine,
As my small Cruse best fits my little Wine. ·

2. A little Seed best fits a little Soyle,
   A little Trade best fits a little Toyle :
As my small Jarre best fits my little Oyle.

3. A little Bin best fits a little Bread,
   A little Garland fits a little Head :
As my small stuffe best fits my little Shed.

4. A little Hearth best fits a little Fire,
   A little Chappell fits a little Quire,
As my small Bell [3] best fits my little Spire.

[3] The tower of Herrick's church of Dean Priory still remains, but the bells are comparatively modern (1734).

5. A little streame best fits a little Boat ;
    A little lead best fits a little Float ;[4]
    As my small Pipe best fits my little note.

6. A little meat best fits a little bellie,
    As sweetly, Lády, give me leave to tell ye,
    This little pipkin fits this little Jellie.

Upon the Roses in Julia's *bosome.*

THRICE happie Roses, so much grac't, to have
    Within the Bosome of my Love your grave.
Die when ye will, your sepulchre is knowne,
Your Grave her bosome is, the Lawne the Stone.

Maids nay's are nothing.[5]

MAIDS nay's are nothing, they are shie
    But to desire what they denie.

The smell of the Sacrifice.

THE Gods require the thighes
    Of Beeves for sacrifice ;
Which rosted, we the steam
Must sacrifice to them :
Who though they do not eat,
Yet love the smell of meat.

---

[4] Used in angling.   [5] See Glossarial Index s. v.

Lovers how they come and part.

A *GYGES* Ring [6] they beare about them still,
  To be, and not seen when and where they will.
They tread on clouds, and though they sometimes fall,
They fall like dew, but make no noise at all.
So silently they one to th' other come,
As colours steale into the Peare or Plum,
And Aire-like, leave no pression [7] to be seen
Where e're they met, or parting place has been.

To women, to hide their Teeth, if they be rotten or rusty.

C LOSE keep your lips, if that you meane
  To be accounted inside cleane :
For if you cleave them, we shall see
There in your teeth much Leprosie.

In praise of women.

O *JUPITER,* sho'd I speake ill
  Of woman-kind, first die I will ;
Since that I know, 'mong all the rest
Of creatures, woman is the best.

---

[6] See Plato's Republic, ii.   [7] = impression.

The Apron of Flowers.

TO gather Flowers *Sappha* went,
    And homeward she did bring
Within her Lawnie Continent,[8]
    The treasure of the Spring.

She smiling blusht, and blushing smil'd,
    And sweetly blushing thus,
She lookt as she'd been got with child
    By young *Favonius.*[9]

Her Apron gave (as she did passe)
    An Odor more divine,
More pleasing too, then ever was   [*than*
    The lap of *Proserpine.*[1]

The Candor [2] of Julias teeth.

WHITE as *Zenobias* teeth, the which the Girles
    Of Rome did weare for their most precious
      Pearles.[3]

[8] = the lawn apron containing the "treasure of the Spring." See Glossarial Index s. v.

[9] ———— "Time will run
On smoother, till Favonius re-inspire
The frózen earth." (Milton : Sonnet xx).

[1] She was gathering flowers when carried off.

[2] = whiteness.   [3] Mythical.

Upon her weeping.

SHE wept upon her cheeks, and weeping so,
  She seem'd to quench loves fires that there did
      glow.

Another upon her weeping.

SHE by the River sate, and sitting there,
  She wept, and made it deeper by a teare.

Delay.

BREAK off Delay, since we but read of one
  That ever prosper'd by *Cunctation.*[4]

To Sir John Berkley, *Governour of Exeter.*[5]

STAND forth, brave man, since fate has made
      thee here.
The *Hector* over *Agèd Exeter;*

[4] i. e. Fabius Maximus, Cunctatus.

[5] Youngest son of Sir Maurice Berkeley, by Elizabeth, d. of Sir Henry Killigrew.   His loyalty was so appreciated by the Queen that she went to Exeter, while he was Governor there, to be under his protection during her accouchement, and the Princess Henrietta Maria was born there.   He subsequently shared the exile of the royal family, and was created by Charles II. 19th May, 1658, Baron Berkeley, of Stratton, co. Somerset.   He died 28th August, 1678.

Who for a long sad time has weeping stood,
Like a *poore Lady* lost in Widdowhood :
But feares not now to see her safety sold [6]
(As other Townes and Cities were) for gold,
By those ignoble *Births*, which shame the stem
That gave Progermination[7] unto them :
Whose restlesse *Ghosts* shall heare their children sing.
Our Sires betraid their Countrey and their King.
True, if this Citie seven times rounded was
With rock, and seven times circumflankt with brasse,
Yet if thou wert not, *Berkley*, loyall proofe,
The Senators down tumbling with the Roofe,
Would into prais'd (but pitied) ruines fall,
Leaving no shew, where stood the *Capitoll.*
But thou art just and itchlesse,[8] and dost please
Thy *Genius* with two strength'ning *Buttresses*,
Faith, and *Affection :* which will never slip
To weaken this thy great *Dictator-ship.*

To Electra. *Love looks for Love.*

LOVE love begets ; then never be
    Unsoft to him who's smooth to thee.

---

[6] See Glossarial Index, ' postern bribe.'
[7] = budding forth or branching out.
[8] i. e. no ' itching palm ' for bribes.

Tygers and Beares (I've heard some say)
For profer'd love will love repay : [9]
None are so harsh, but if they find
Softnesse in others, will be kind ;
Affection will affection move,
Then you must like, because I love.

Regression spoiles Resolution.

H AST thou attempted greatnesse ? then go on,
  Back-turning slackens Resolution.

Contention.

D ISCREET and prudent we that Discord call,
  That either profits, or not hurts at all.

Consultation.

C ONSULT ere thou begin'st, that done, go on
  With all wise speed for execution.

Love dislikes nothing.

W HATSOEVER thing I see,
      Rich or poore although it be ;
  'Tis a Mistresse unto mee.

[9] Legends of these abound everywhere.

Be my Girle, or faire or browne,
Do's she smile, or do's she frowne :
Still I write a Sweet-heart downe.

Be she rough, or smooth of skin ;
When I touch, I then begin
For to let Affection in.

Be she bald, or do's she weare
Locks incurl'd of other haire ;
I shall find enchantment there.

Be she whole, or be she rent,
So my fancie be content,
She's to me most excellent.

Be she fat, or be she leane,
Be she sluttish, be she cleane,
I'm a man for ev'ry Sceane.[1]

Our own sinnes unseen.

OTHER mens sins wee ever beare in mind ;
None sees the fardell [2] *of his faults behind.*

---

[1] See Glossarial Index s. v.
[2]   " Suus quoique attributus est error :
          Sed non videmus manticæ quod in tergo est."
Catullus xvi. 20, 21 : Cf. Persius iv. 23. = Burden or pack.

No Paines, no Gaines.

IF little labour, little are our gaines :
  Mans fortunes are according to his paines.

Upon Slouch.

SLOUCH he packs up, and goes to sev'rall Faires,
  And weekly Markets for to sell his wares :
Meane time that he from place to place do's rome,
His wife her owne ware sells as fast at home.

Vertue best united.

BY so much, vertue is the lesse,
  By how much, neere to singlenesse.

The eye.

A WANTON and lascivious eye
  Betrayes the Hearts Adulterie.

To Prince Charles upon his coming to Exeter.[3]

WHAT Fate decreed, Time now ha's made us see
  A Renovation of the West by Thee.
That Preternaturall Fever, which did threat
Death to our Countrey, now hath lost his heat :

---

[3] Prince Charles, afterwards Charles II., " went from Launceston
o Exeter in one day," on Friday, Aug. 29th, 1645. Clarendon ix. 81.

And calmes succeeding, we perceive no more
Th' unequall Pulse to beat, as heretofore.
Something there yet remaines for Thee to do ;
Then reach those ends that thou wast destin'd to.
Go on with *Sylla's* Fortune ; let thy Fate
Make Thee like Him, this, that way fortunate :
Apollos Image side with Thee to blesse
Thy Warre (discreetly made) with white[4] successe.
Meane time thy Prophets Watch by Watch shall pray ;
While young *Charles* fights, and fighting wins the
        day.
That done, our smooth-pac't Poems all shall be
Sung in the high *Doxologie* of Thee.
Then maids shall strew Thee, and thy Curles from
        them
Receive (with Songs) a flowrie Diadem.

A Song.

BURNE, or drowne me, choose ye whether,
    So I may but die together :
Thus to slay me by degrees,
Is the height of Cruelties.
What needs twenty stabs, when one
Strikes me dead as any stone ?

[4] See Glossarial Index s. v.

O shew mercy then, and be
Kind at once to murder mee.

Princes and Favourites.[5]

PRINCES and Fav'rites are most deere, while they
  By giving and receiving hold the play :
But the Relation then of both growes poor,
When these can aske, and Kings can give no more.

Examples, or like Prince, like People.

EXAMPLES lead us, and wee likely see,
  Such as the Prince is, will his People be.

Potentates.

LOVE and the *Graces* evermore do wait
  Upon the man that is a Potentate.

The Wake.[6]

COME *Anthea* let us two
  Go to Feast, as others do.
Tarts and Custards, Creams and Cakes,
Are the Junketts[7] still at Wakes :

[5] " *Rex vult honesta, nemo non eadem volet.*"
[6] = Feast.   Still used in this sense in Devonshire and elsewhere.
[7] See Glossarial Index s. v.

Unto which the Tribes resort,
Where the businesse is the sport:
Morris-dancers thou shalt see,
Marian[8] too in Pagentrie :
And a Mimick to devise
Many grinning properties.
Players there will be, and those
Base in action as in clothes :
Yet with strutting they will please
The incurious[9] Villages.
Neer the dying of the day,
There will be a *Cudgell*-Play,
Where a *Coxcomb* will be broke,
Ere a good *word* can be spoke :
But the anger ends all here,
Drencht in Ale, or drown'd in Beere.
Happy Rusticks, best content
With the cheapèst Merriment :
And possesse no other feare,
Then to want the Wake next Yeare.   [*than*

The Peter-*penny*.

FRESH strowings allow
To my Sepulcher now,

[8] Ibid.   [9] = careless, not over-nice, and therefore easily pleased.

To make my lodging the sweeter ;
    A staffe or a wand
    Put then in my hand,
With a pennie to pay S. *Peter.*[1]

    Who has not a Crosse,
    Must sit with the losse,
And no whit further must venture ;
    Since the Porter he
    Will paid have his fee,
Or els not one there must enter.

    Who at a dead lift,
    Can't send for a gift
A Pig to the Priest for a Roster,
    Shall heare his Clarke say,
    By yea and by nay,
No pennie, no Pater Noster.

To Doctor Alablaster.[2]

NOR art thou lesse esteem'd, that I have plac'd
    (Amongst mine honour'd) Thee (almost) the
        last :

---

[1] The Romish version of the Charon fee.

[2] See my memoir of him in the new edition of the Encycl. Britannica s. n. : born 1567 : died 1640. The allusions are to his now forgotten work on the Book of Revelation, Daniel, &c., &c.

In great Processions many lead the way
To him, who is the triumph of the day,
As these have done to Thee, who art the one,
One onely glory of a million :
In whom the spirit of the Gods do's dwell,
Firing thy soule, by which thou dost foretell
When this or that vast *Dinastie* must fall
Downe to a *Fillit* more *Imperiall.*
When this or that *Horne* shall be broke, and when
Others shall spring up in their place agen :
When times and seasons and all yeares must lie
Drown'd in the Sea of wild Eternitie :
When the *Black Dooms-day Bookes* (as yet unseal'd)
Shall by the mighty *Angell* be reveal'd :
And when the Trumpet which thou late hast found
Shall call to Judgment ; tell us when the sound
Of this or that great Aprill day[3] shall be,
And next the Gospell wee will credit thee.
Meane time like Earth-wormes we will craule below,
And wonder at Those Things that thou dost know.

Upon his Kinswoman Mrs. M. S.

HERE lies a Virgin, and as sweet
    As ere was wrapt in winding sheet.

---

[3] Cf. Glossarial Index s. v. = day of rain and sunshine, weal and woe : or simply, day of tears.

Her name if next you wo'd have knowne,
The Marble speaks it *Mary Stone :* [4]
Who dying in her blooming yeares,
This Stone, for names sake, melts to teares.
If fragrant Virgins you'l but keep
A Fast, while Jets and Marbles weep,
And praying, strew some Roses on her,
You'l do my *Neice* abundant honour.

Felicitie knowes no Fence.

OF both our Fortunes good and bad we find
Prosperitie more searching of the mind :
Felicitie flies o're the Wall and Fence,
While misery keeps in with patience.

Death ends all woe.

TIME is the Bound of things, where e're we go,
Fate gives a meeting. Death's the end of woe.

A Conjuration, to Electra.

BY those soft *Tods* of wooll [5]
With which the aire is full :
By all those Tinctures there,
That paint the *Hemisphere :*

---

[4] See Memorial-Introduction.   [5] = gossamer threads.

By Dewes and drisling Raine,
That swell the Golden Graine :
By all those sweets that be
I' th flowrie Nunnerie :
By silent Nights, and the
Three Formes of *Heccate :*
By all Aspects [6] that blesse
The sober *Sorceresse,*
While juice she straines, and pith [7]
To make her Philters with :
By Time, that hastens on
Things to perfection :
And by your self, the best
Conjurement of the rest :
O my *Electra !* be
In love with none, but me.

Courage cool'd.

I CANNOT love, as I have lov'd before :
For I'm grown old ; &, with mine age, grown
   poore :

---

[6] Astrological term : ━ the position of one planet in reference to
another, of which reckoned by distance there were five.

[7] ━ as of rushes. Here, the strength, substance, or quintessence
of anything.

Love must be fed by wealth : this blood of mine
Must needs wax cold, if wanting bread and wine.

The Spell.

HOLY Water come and bring ;
   Cast in Salt, for seasoning :
Set the Brush for sprinkling :
Sacred Spittle bring ye hither ;
Meale and it now mix together ;
And a little Oyle to either : [8]
Give the Tapers here their light,
Ring the *Saints-Bell,*[9] to affright
Far from hence the evill Sp'rite.

His wish to privacie.

GIVE me a Cell
   To dwell,
Where no foot hath
   A path :
There will I spend,
   And end
My wearied yeares
   In teares.

[8] Folk-lore.   [9] See Glossarial Index s. v.

A good Husband.[1]

A MASTER of a house (as I have read)
    Must be the first man up, and last in bed :
With the Sun rising he must walk his grounds ;
See this, View that, and all the other bounds :
Shut every gate ; mend every hedge that's torne,
Either with old, or plant therein new thorne :
Tread ore his gleab, but with such care, that where
He sets his foot, he leaves rich *compost*[2] there.

A *Hymne to* Bacchus.

I SING thy praise *Iacchus,*
    Who with thy *Thyrse* dost thwack us :
And yet thou so dost back us
With boldnesse, that we feare
No *Brutus* entring here ;
Nor *Cato* the severe.[3]
What though the *Lictors* threat us,
We know they dare not beate us ;
So long as thou dost heat us.
When we thy *Orgies* sing,
Each Cobler is a King ;
Nor dreads he any thing :

---

[1] =husband-man.   [2] See Glossarial Index s. v.
[3] See Glossarial Index s. v.

And though he doe not rave,

Yet he'l the courage have

To call my *Lord Maior* knave ;

Besides too, in a brave,

Although he has no riches,

But walks with dangling breeches,

And skirts that want their stiches,

And shewes his naked flitches ;

Yet he'le be thought or seen,

So good as *George-a-Green ;* [4]

And calls his Blouze, his Queene ;

And speaks in language keene :

O *Bacchus !* let us be

From cares and troubles free ;

And thou shalt heare how we

Will chant new *Hymnes* to thee.

---

[4] The poet, in this line, seems to have a reference to the following passage in the old anonymous comedy, *George a Green, Pinner of Wakefield :*

CUDDY.

——Had King James been as good as George a Greene,
Yet Billy Musgrove would have fought with him.

EDWARD.

As George a Greene !
I pray thee, Cuddy, let me question thee.
Much have I heard, since I came to my crown,
Many in manner of proverb say,
" Were he *as good as George a Greene*, I would shake him sure."

For what concerns that noted outlaw Robin Hood, and George the

Upon Pusse *and her Prentice.   Epig.*

PUSSE and her Prentice both at Draw-gloves
    play ; [5]
That done, they kisse, and so draw out the day :
At night they draw to Supper ; then well fed,
They draw their clothes off both, so draw to bed.

Blame the reward of Princes.

AMONG disasters that discention brings,
    This not the least is, which belongs to Kings.
If Wars goe well ; each for a part layes claime :
If ill, then Kings, not Souldiers beare the blame.

Pinner, in this comedy, the reader is referred to a ballad in Evans'
Collection of Old Ballads, Vol. I., page 99, which is mentioned by
Drayton, in his *Polyolbion,* Song 28.   Richard Braithwaite also
notices the subject, in his *Strappado for the Devil,* 1615, 8vo : page
203.   Pinner, or *pinder,* it may here be proper to remark, signifies
warden of the pinfold.   Mr. Steevens, who wrote at a very recent
period, observed that the figure of this rustic hero, George a Greene,
was still preserved on a sign at the bottom of Gray's Inn Lane.
See Dodsley's *Collection of Old Plays,* Vol. 3.   N.   The prowess of
this ballad-hero was so well known that it can only be said that both
Herrick and the author of the comedy make use of a proverbial
saying.
   [5] See Glossarial-Index s. v.

Clemency in Kings.

KINGS must not only cherish up the good,
　But must be niggards of the meanest bloud.

Anger.

WRONGS, if neglected, vanish in short time,
　But heard with anger, we confesse the crime.

A Psalme or Hymne to the Graces.

GLORY be to the Graces !
　That doe in publike places,
Drive thence what ere encumbers,
The listning to my numbers.

Honour be to the Graces !
Who doe with sweet embraces,
Shew they are well contented
With what I have invented.

Worship be to the Graces !
Who do from sowre faces,
And lungs that wo'd infect me,
For evermore protect me.

An Hymne to the Muses.

HONOUR to you who sit !
　Neere to the well of wit ;
And drink your fill of it.

Glory and worship be !
To you, sweet Maids (thrice three)
Who still inspire me.

And teach me how to sing
Unto the *Lyrick* string,
My measures ravishing.

Then while I sing your praise,
My *Priest-hood* crown with bayes
Green, to the end of dayes.

Upon Julia's *Clothes.*

WHENAS in silks my *Julia* goes,
    Then, then (me thinks) how sweetly flowes
That liquefaction of her clothes.

Next, when I cast mine eyes and see
That brave Vibration each way free ;
O how that glittering taketh me !

Moderation.

IN things a moderation keepe,
   Kings ought to sheare, not skin their sheepe.

To Anthea.

LETS call for *Hymen* if agreed thou art ;
   Delays in love but crucifie the heart.

Loves thornie Tapers yet neglected lye :
Speak thou the word, they'l kindle by and by.
The nimble howers wooe us on to wed,
And *Genius*[6] waits to have us both to bed.
Behold, for us the *Naked Graces* stay
With maunds [7] of roses for to strew the way :
Besides, the most religious Prophet stands
Ready to joyne, as well our hearts as hands.
Juno yet smiles ; but if she chance to chide,
Ill luck 'twill bode to th' Bridegroome and the Bride.
Tell me *Anthea*, dost thou fondly dread
The loss of that we call a Maydenhead ?
Come, Ile instruct thee.   Know, the vestall fier
Is not by mariage quencht, but flames the higher.

Upon Prew *his Maid.*

I N this little Urne is laid
        Prewdence[8] *Baldwin* (once my maid)
From whose happy spark here let
Spring the purple Violet.

The Invitation.

T O sup with thee thou didst me home invite ;
        And mad'st a promise that mine appetite

---

[6] = Herrick's use of and for Lar.   [7] = baskets.   See Glossarial Index s. v.   [8] Was there an intended pun on ' Prew ' or ' Prue ' in ' Prewdence ' ?

Sho'd meet and tire, on such lautitious [9] meat,
The like not *Heliogabalus* did eat :
And richer Wine wo'dst give to me (thy guest)
Then Roman *Sylla* powr'd out at his feast.   [*than*
I came ; (tis true) and lookt for Fowle of price,
The bastard *Phenix* [1] ; bird of *Paradice ;*
And for no less then Aromatick Wine
Of *Maydens-blush,* [2] commixt with *Jessimine.*
Cleane was the herth, the mantle [3] larded jet ; [4]
Which wanting *Lar,* [5] and smoke, hung weeping wet ;
At last, i' th' noone of winter, did appeare
A ragd-soust-neats-foot with sick vineger :
And in a burnisht Flagonet stood by
Beere small as Comfort, dead as Charity.
At which amaz'd, and pondring on the food,
How cold it was, and how it child my blood ;
I curst the master; and I damn'd the souce [6] ;
And swore I'de got the ague of the house.

---

[9] Dainty = "*epulae dulces*": Horace, Od. iii. 8, 6.   [1] Why 'bastard'?   [2] A flower. See Glossarial Index s. v.

[3] 'mantle' = mantle-piece. See Glossarial Index s. v.

[4] 'larded jet' = to 'lard' is to mix fat or fatty flesh with lean or dry meat : and here Herrick means greasily flaked or streaked, not merely with smoke, but with soot.   [5] Here = the household fire.

[6] = sauce (as of pickles).

Well, when to eat thou dost me next desire,
I'le bring a Fever; since thou keep'st no fire.

Ceremonies for Christmasse.

COME, bring with a noise,
 My merrie merrie boyes,
The Christmas Log to the firing;
 While my good Dame, she
 Bids ye all be free;
And drink to your hearts desiring.

 With the last yeeres brand
 Light the new block, And
For good successe in his spending,
 On your Psaltries play,
 That sweet luck may
Come while the Log is a-teending.[7]

 Drink now the strong Beere,
 Cut the white loafe here,
The while the meat is a-shredding;
 For the rare Mince-Pie
 And the Plums stand by
To fill the Paste that's a-kneading.

---

[7] = kindling. A word of Saxon derivation. N. In some parts of Devonshire an ashen faggot was burnt instead of a yule-log. 'Teen' is still used for, to kindle, light, burn.

Christmasse-Eve, another Ceremonie.

COME guard this night the Christmas-Pie,
  That the Thiefe, though ne'r so slie,
With his Flesh-hooks, don't come nie
      To catch it

From him, who all alone sits there,
Having his eyes still in his eare,
And a deale of nightly feare
      To watch it.

Another to the Maids.

WASH your hands, or else the fire
  Will not teend [8] to your desire ;
Unwasht hands, ye Maidens, know,
Dead [9] the Fire, though ye blow.

Another.

WASSAILE the Trees,[1] that they may beare
  You many a Plum, and many a Peare :
For more or lesse fruits they will bring,
As you doe give them Wassailing.

---

[8] =kindle, or burn, as before. sarial Index for other examples.

[9] A verb=deaden. See Glos-
[1] Query—Folk-lore ?

Power and Peace.

'TIS *never, or but seldome knowne,*
　Power and Peace to keep one Throne.

To his deare Valentine, Mistresse Margaret Falconbrige.[1]

NOW is your turne (my Dearest) to be set
　A Jem in this eternall Coronet :
'Twas rich before; but since your Name is downe,
It sparkles now like *Ariadne's* Crowne.
Blaze by this Sphere for ever : Or this doe,
Let Me and It shine evermore by you.

To Oenone.

SWEET *Oenone,* doe but say
　Love thou dost, though Love sayes Nay.
Speak me faire ; for Lovers be
Gently kill'd by Flatterie.

Verses.

WHO will not honour Noble Numbers, when
　Verses out-live the bravest deeds of men ?

---

[1] A now forgotten Devonshire beauty.

Happinesse.

THAT Happines do's still the longest thrive,
  Where Joyes and Griefs have Turns Alternative.

Things of choice, long a comming.

WE pray 'gainst Warre, yet we enjoy no Peace ;
  Desire deferr'd is, that it may encrease.

Poetry perpetuates the Poet.

HERE I my selfe might likewise die,
  And utterly forgotten lye,
But that eternall Poetrie
Repullulation [2] gives me here
Unto the thirtieth thousand yeere,
When all now dead shall re-appeare.

Upon Bice.

B*ICE* laughs, when no man speaks ; and doth
  protest
It is his own breech there that breaks the jest.

---

[2] = re-budding, re-juvenescence.

Upon Trencherman.

TOM shifts the Trenchers ; yet he never can
    Endure that luke-warme name of Serving-man :
Serve or not serve, let *Tom* doe what he can,
He is a serving, who's a Trencher-man.

Kisses.

GIVE me the food that satisfies a Guest :
    Kisses are but dry banquets to a Feast.

Orpheus.

O*RPHEUS* he went (as Poets tell)
    To fetch *Euridice* from Hell ;[3]
And had her ; but it was upon
This short but strict condition :
Backward he should not looke while he
Led her through Hells obscuritie :
But ah ! it hapnèd as he made
His passage through that dreadfull shade :
Revolve he did his loving eye ;
(For gentle feare, or jelousie)
And looking back, that look did sever
Him and *Euridice* for ever.

[3] e. g. Virgil : Georgic IV.

Upon Comely *a good speaker but an ill Singer. Epig.*

C OMELY Acts well ; and when he speaks his part,
 He doth it with the sweetest tones of Art :
But when he sings a *Psalme*, ther's none can be
More curst for singing out of tune then he.   [*than*

Any Way for wealth.

E'ENE all Religious courses to be rich
 Hath been reherst, by *Joell Michelditch :*[4]
But now perceiving that it still do's please
The sterner Fates, to cross his purposes ;
He tacks about, and now he doth profess
Rich he will be by all unrighteousness :
Thus if our ship fails of her Anchor hold,
We'l love the Divell, so he lands the gold.

Upon an old Woman.

O LD Widdow *Prouse* to do her neighbours evill ·
 Wo'd give (some say) her soule unto the
   Devill.
Well, when sh'as kild that Pig, Goose, Cock or Hen,
What wo'd she give to get that soule agen ?

***

[4] A Devonshire name.

Upon Pearch.   *Epig.*

THOU writes in Prose, how sweet all Virgins be ;
But ther's not one, doth praise the smell of
    thee.

To Sapho.

SAPHO, I will chuse to go
    Where the Northern Winds do blow
Endlesse Ice, and endlesse Snow :
Rather then I once wo'd see,   [*than*
But a Winters face in thee,
To benumme my hopes and me.

To his faithfull friend, Master John Crofts, *Cup-bearer to the King.*[5]

FOR all thy many courtesies to me,
    Nothing I have (my *Crofts*) to send to Thee
For the requitall ; save this only one
Halfe of my just remuneration.
For since I've travail'd all this Realm throughout
To seeke, and find some few *Immortals* out

---

[5] He was 3rd son of Sir John Crofts, of Saxham, co. Suffolk, by
Mary, d. of Sir Thomas Shirley, Kt. of co. Suffolk.   He was buried
at Saxham 23rd June, 1664.

To *circumspangle* [6] this my spacious Sphere,
(As Lamps for everlasting shining here :)
And having fixt Thee in mine Orbe a Starre,
(Amongst the rest) both bright and singular ;
The present Age will tell the world thou art
If not to th' whole, yet satisfy'd in part.
As for the rest, being too great a summe .
Here to be paid ; Ile pay't i'th'world to come.

The Bride-Cake.

THIS day my *Julia* thou must make
  For Mistresse Bride, the wedding Cake :
Knead but the Dow, and it will be
To paste of Almonds turn'd by thee :
Or kisse it thou, but once, or twice,
And for the Bride-Cake ther'l be Spice.

To be merry.

LETS now take our time ;
  While w'are in our Prime ;
And old, old Age is a-farre off :
  For the evill evill dayes
  Will come on apace ;
Before we can be aware of.

[6] See Glossarial Index for other coinages with 'circum.'

Buriall.

MAN may want Land to live in ; but for all,
  Nature finds out some place for buriall.

Lenitie.

TIS the Chyrurgions praise, and height of Art,
  Not to cut off, but cure the vicious part.

Penitence.

WHO after his transgression doth repent,
  Is halfe, or altogether innocent.

Griefe.

CONSIDER sorrowes, how they are aright :
  Griefe, if't be great, 'tis short ; if long, 'tis light.

The Maiden-blush.

SO look the mornings when the Sun
    Paints them with fresh Vermilion :
So Cherries blush, and Kathern Peares,[7]
And Apricocks, in youthfull yeares :
So Corrolls looke more lovely Red,
And Rubies lately polishèd :

[7] A famous pear—still known by the Saint's name.

So purest Diaper doth shine,
Stain'd by the Beames of Clarret wine :   .
As *Julia* looks when she doth dress
Her either cheeke with bashfullness.

The Meane.

I*MPARITIE doth ever discord bring :*
The Mean the Musique makes in every_thing.[8]

Haste hurtfull.

H*ASTE is unhappy : what we Rashly do*
Is both unluckie ; I,[9] *and foolish too.*
Where War with rashnesse is attempted, there
The soldiers leave the Field with equall feare.

Purgatory.

R EADERS, wee entreat ye pray
For the soule of *Lucia ;*
That in little time she be
From her *Purgatory* free :
In th' *intrim* she desires
That your teares may coole her fires.

---

[8] Hesiod.

[9] =aye.   See Glossarial Index for other examples of this, the
contemporary spelling.

The Cloud.

SEEST thou that Cloud that rides in State [1]
  Part *Ruby-like*, part *Candidate ?*[2]
It is no other then the Bed   [*than*
Where *Venus* sleeps (halfe smother**è**d.)

Upon Loach.

SEEAL'D up with Night-gum, Loach each morn-
      ing lyes,
Till his Wife licking, so unglews his eyes.
No question then, but such a lick is sweet,
When a warm tongue do's with such Ambers meet.

The Amber Bead.

I SAW a Flie within a Beade
  Of Amber cleanly buri**è**d :
The Urne was little, but the room
  More rich then *Cleopatra's* Tombe.[3]   [*than*

To my dearest Sister M. Mercie Herrick.

WHENERE I go, or what so ere befalls
  Me in mine Age, or forraign Funerals,

---

[1] Perhaps in double sense of ' in majesty ' and ' canopy-like ' :
' state ' meaning a canopy.   [2] = white, whitened.
[3] See Memorial-Introduction on this in relation to the Lines
ascribed to Milton (1868) by Professor Morley.

This Blessing I will leave thee, ere I go,
Prosper thy Basket, and therein thy Dow.
Feed on the paste of Filberts, or else knead
And Bake the floure of Amber for thy bread.
Balm may thy Trees drop, and thy Springs runne
    oyle,
And everlasting Harvest crown thy Soile !
These I but wish for ; but thy selfe shall see,
The blessing fall in mellow times on Thee.

The Transfiguration.

IMMORTALL clothing I put on,
   So soone as *Julia* I am gon
To mine eternall Mansion.

Thou, thou art here, to humane sight
Cloth'd all with incorrupted light ;
But yet how more admir'dly bright

Wilt thou appear, when thou art set
In thy refulgent Thronelet,[4]
That shin'st thus in thy counterfeit ?

---

[4] Diminutive of 'throne.'

Suffer that thou canst not shift.

DO'S Fortune rend thee?   Beare with thy hard
  Fate :
Vertuous instructions ne'r are delicate.
Say, do's she frown? still countermand her threats :
Vertue best loves those children that she beates.

To the Passenger.

IF I lye unburied Sir,
   These my Reliques, (pray) interre :
'Tis religious part to see
Stones, or turfes to cover me.
One word more I had to say ;
But it skills not ; go your way ;
He that wants a buriall roome
For a Stone, ha's Heaven his Tombe.

Upon Nodes.

WHEREVER Nodes do's in the Summer come,
   He prayes his Harvest may be well brought
      home.
What store of Corn has carefull *Nodes*, thinke you,
Whose Field his foot is, and whose Barn his shooe?

TO THE KING,
Upon his taking of *Leicester.*[5]

THIS Day is Yours, *Great* CHARLES ! and in this
    War
Your Fate, and Ours, alike Victorious are.
In her white Stole, now Victory do's rest
Enspher'd with Palm on Your Triumphant Crest.
Fortune is now Your Captive ; other Kings
Hold but her hands ; You hold both hands and wings.

To Julia, *in her Dawn, or Day-breake.*

BY the next kindling of the day
    My *Julia* thou shalt see,
Ere *Ave-Mary* thou canst say
    Ile come and visit thee.

Yet ere thou counsel'st with thy Glasse,
    Appeare thou to mine eyes
As smooth, and nak't, as she that was
    The prime of *Paradice.*

If blush thou must, then blush thou through
    A Lawn, that thou mayst looke

---

[5] Leicester was stormed May 31, 1645, at the beginning of the campaign, which came to so speedy a close at Naseby.

As purest Pearles, or Pebles do
    When peeping through a Brooke.

As Lillies shrin'd in Christall, so
    Do thou to me appeare ;
Or Damask Roses when they grow
    To sweet acquaintance there.

Counsell.

'TWAS *Cesars* saying : *Kings no lesse Conquerors
    are*
By their wise Counsell, then they be by Warre.[6]   [*than*

Bad Princes pill[7] their People.

LIKE those infernall Deities which eate
    The best of all the sacrific̀d meate ;
And leave their servants, but the smoak & sweat :
So many *Kings*, and *Primates*[8] too there are,
Who claim the Fat, and Fleshie for their share,
And leave their subjects but the starv̀d ware.

Most Words, lesse Workes.

IN desp'rate cases, all, or most are known
    Commanders, *few for execution.*

---

[6] Where ?   [7] = peel, strip, spoil.
[8] Herrick could hit dignitaries.

To Dianeme.

I CO'D but see thee yesterday
  Stung by a fretfull Bee ;
And I the Javelin suckt away,
  And heal'd the wound in thee.

A thousand thorns, and Bryars & Stings,
  I have in my poore Brest ;
Yet ne'r can see that salve which brings
  My Passions any rest.

As Love shall helpe me, I admire
  How thou canst sit and smile,
To see me bleed, and not desire
  To stench⁹ the blood the while.

If thou compos'd of gentle mould
  Art so unkind to me ;
What dismall Stories will be told
  Of those that cruell be ?

Upon Tap.

1P (better known then trusted) as we heare, [*than*
Sold his old Mothers Spectacles for Beere :

⁹ = staunch.

And not unlikely; rather too then fail,   [*than*
He'l sell her Eyes, and Nose, for Beere and Ale.

His Losse.

ALL has been plundered from me, but my wit
  Fortune her selfe can lay no claim to it.

Draw, and Drinke.

MILK stil your Fountains, and your Springs, for
    why?
The more th'are drawn, the lesse they wil grow dry.

Upon Punchin.   *Epig.*

GIVE me a reason why men call
    Punchin a dry *plant-animall.*
Because as Plants by water grow,
Punchin by Beere and Ale, spreads so.

To Oenone.

THOU sayest Loves Dart
      Hath prickt thy heart;
And thou do'st languish too :
      If one poore prick,
      Can make thee sick,
.Say, what wo'd many do ?

Upon Blinks. *Epig.*

TOM *BLINKS* his Nose, is full of wheales,[10] and
these
Tom calls not pimples, but *Pimpleides :*[1]
Sometimes (in mirth) he sayes each whelk's a sparke
(When drunke with Beere) to light him home, i'th'
dark.

Upon Adam Peapes.[2] *Epig.*

PEAPES he do's strut, and pick his Teeth, as if
His jawes had tir'd on some large Chine of
Beefe.
But nothing so : the Dinner *Adam* had,
Was cheese full ripe with Teares,[3] with Bread as sad.[4]

To Electra.

SHALL I go to Love and tell,
Thou art all turn'd isicle ?

---

[10] The word may mean a postule or vesicle ; but here it is explained
in next and l. 3 as a pimple and whelk (the latter a knob like the
shell fish, so named from its shape). [2] Pun on the ' Pleiades.'

[1] A Devonshire name.

[3] = thin and watery. [4] dark brown or blackish, and not
' risen,' (besides the equivoque).

Shall I say her [5] Altars be
Disadorn'd, and scorn'd by thee?
O beware! in time submit;
Love has yet no wrathfull fit:
If her patience turns to ire,
Love is then consuming fire.

To Mistresse Amie Potter. [6]

A I me! I love, give him your hand to kisse
    Who both your wooer and your Poet is.
Nature has pre-compos'd us both to Love;
Your part's to grant; my Scean must be to move.
Deare, can you like, and liking love your Poet?
If you say (I) [7] Blush-guiltinesse will shew it.
Mine eyes must wooe you, (though I sigh the while)
True Love is tonguelesse as a Crocodile. [8]
And you may find in Love these differing parts;
Wooers have Tongues of Ice, but burning hearts.

---

[5] It would seem that the poet has here chosen to personify Love as a female, which is a novelty. The word *her* occurring both in the third and seventh line leaves no room to suppose a misprint. N. It is simply = Venus the goddess of Love.

[6] One of the daughters of the Bishop of Carlisle. See Memorial-Introduction.   [7] = aye.   [8] A "vulgar error."

Upon a Maide.

HERE she lyes (in Bed of Spice)
    Faire as *Eve* in Paradice :
For her beauty it was such
Poets co'd not praise too much.
Virgins come, and in a Ring
Her supreamest *Requiem* sing ;
Then depart, but see ye tread
Lightly, lightly ore the dead.

Upon Love.

LOVE is a Circle, and an Endlesse Sphere ;
    From good to good, revolving here, & there.

Beauty.

BEAUTI'S no other but a lovely Grace
    Of lively colours, flowing from the face.

Upon Love.

SOME salve to every sore, we may apply ;
    Only for my wound there's no remedy.
Yet if my *Julia* kisse me, there will be
A soveraign balme found out to cure ⁹ me

⁹ Apparently dissyllabic.

Upon Hanch *a Schoolmaster.   Epig.*

H*ANCH,* since he (lately) did interre his wife,
　　He weepes and sighs (as weary of his life.)
Say, is 't for reall griefe he mourns ? not so ;
Teares have their springs from joy, as well as woe.

Upon Peason.   *Epig.*

L ONG Locks of late our Zelot *Peason* weares,
　　Not for to hide his high and mighty eares ;
No, but because he wo'd not have it seen,
That Stubble stands, where once large eares have
　　been.[1]

To his Booke.

M AKE haste away, and let one be
　　A friendly Patron unto thee :
Lest rapt from hence, I see thee lye
Torn for the use of Pasterie :
Or see thy injur'd Leaves serve well,
To make loose Gownes for Mackarell :[2]
Or see the Grocers in a trice,
Make hoods [3] of thee to serve out Spice.[4]

---

[1] = had been pilloried and ear-shorn.
[2] Fish so named.   [3] Bags or pokes.   [4] These remind me of

Readinesse.

THE readinesse of doing, doth expresse
No other, but the doers willingnesse.

Writing.

WHEN words we want, Love teacheth to
endite ;
And what we blush to speake, she bids us write.

Society.

TWO things do make society to stand ;
The first *Commerce* is, & the next *Command.*

Upon a Maid.

GONE she is a long, long way,
But she has decreed a day
Back to come, (and make no stay.)

some lines I have formerly met with, but where I do not recollect, on
Christmas being a very happy time :
　　　　　" For those who deal in books,
Not sold to readers, but to pastry-cooks :
Learn'd works despis'd by those to merit blind,
They now, well weigh'd, their certain value find.
Blest lot of paper, falsely titled waste,
To wrap those cates which authors seldom taste !
See, on this subject, Catullus, Carmen 90, De Smyrnâ Cinnae :
Martial, Epig. 87, lib. 4 : and Persius, Sat. 1. N. Dr. Nott was
thinking of Dean Donne on Coryat : see my edition of Donne in
Fuller Worthies' Library, Vol. II., pp. 93-96.

So we keepe, till her returne
Here, her ashes, or her Urne.

Satisfaction for sufferings.

FOR all our workes, a recompence is sure :
'Tis sweet to thinke on what was hard t' endure.[5]

The delaying Bride.

WHY so slowly do you move
    To the centre of your love ?
On your niceness though we wait,
Yet the houres say 'tis late :
Coynesse takes us, to a measure ;
But o'racted deads the pleasure.
Go to Bed, and care not when
Cheerfull day shall spring agen.
One *Brave Captain* did command,
(By his word) the Sun to stand :[6]
One short charme if you but say
Will enforce the Moon to stay,
Till you warn her hence (away)
T'ave your blushes seen by day.

[5] " Quod fuit durum pati meminesse dulce est."
[6] Joshua, c. x., v. 13.

To *M*. Henry Lawes, *the excellent*
Composer of his Lyricks.[7]

TOUCH but thy Lire (my *Harrie*) and I heare
    From thee some raptures of the rare *Gotire.*
Then if thy voice commingle with the String,
I heare in thee rare *Laniere* [8] to sing ;
Or curious *Wilson :* [9] Tell me, canst thou be
Less then *Apollo*, that usurp'st such Three ?
Three, unto whom the whole world give applause ;
Yet their Three praises, praise but One ; that's *Lawes.*

Age unfit for Love.

MAIDENS tell me I am old ;
    Let me in my Glasse behold
Whether smooth or not I be,
Or if haire remaines to me.
Well, or be't or be't not so,
This for certainty I know ;
Ill it fits old men to play,
When that Death bids come away.

---

[7] See Memorial-Introduction on these Worthies.
[8] See Glossarial Index s. v.   ' The ' is inserted by press error before Laniere in original text.   [9] See as in 7.

The Bed-man, or Grave-maker.

THOU hast made many Houses for the Dead ;
　　When my Lot calls me to be burièd,
For Love or Pittie, prethee let there be
I'th' Church-yard, made, one Tenement for me.

To Anthea.

A*NTHEA* I am going hence
　　With some small stock of innocence :
But yet those blessed gates I see
Withstanding entrance unto me.
To pray for me doe thou begin,
The Porter then will let me in.

Need.

WHO begs to die for feare of humane need,
　　Wisheth his body, not his soule, good speed.

To Julia.

I AM zeallesse ; prethee pray
　　For my well-fare *(Julia)*
For I thinke the gods require
Male perfumes, but Female fire.[1]

---

[1] Query—Is he playing on the name ' male frankincense ?' and in
' female fire ' is the reference to the vestal fire ?

On Julias *lips.*

SWEET are my *Julia's* lips and cleane,
As if or'ewasht in Hippocrene.[2]

Twilight.

TWILIGHT, no other thing is, Poets say,   [*than*
Then the last part of night, and first of day.[3]

To his Friend, Master J. Jincks.[4]

LOVE, love me now, because I place
Thee here among my righteous race :
The bastard Slips may droop and die
Wanting both Root, and Earth ; but thy
Immortall selfe, shall boldly trust
To live for ever, with my Just.[5]

On himselfe.

IF that my Fate has now fulfill'd my yeere,
And so soone stopt my longer living here ;

---

[2] See Glossarial Index s. v.: the Heliconian fountain.
[3] So Ovid, Amores i. 15, 5, 6 :
  " Qualia sublucent fugiente crepuscula Phœbo :
    Aut ubi nox abiit nec tamen orta dies."
[4] A now forgotten Devonshire friend.
[5] i. e. with my just ones, those of righteous race whom I have celebrated in my verse.

What was't (ye Gods !) a dying man to save,
But while he met with his Paternall grave ;
Though while we living 'bout the world do roame,
We love to rest in peacefull Urnes at home,
Where we may snug, and close together lye
By the dead bones of our deare Ancestrie.

Kings and Tyrants.

'TWIXT Kings & Tyrants there's this difference
    known,
Kings seek their Subjects' good : Tyrants their owne.[6]

Crosses.

OUR Crosses are no other then the rods, [*than*
    And our Diseases, Vultures of the Gods :[7]
Each griefe we feele, that likewise is a Kite
Sent forth by them, our flesh to eate, or bite.

Upon Love.

LOVE brought me to a silent Grove,
    And shew'd me there a Tree,
Where some had hang'd themselves for love,
    And gave a Twist to me.

---

[6] Aristotle, Politics i.   [7] Qu—as of the vulture of Prometheus ?

The Halter was of silk, and gold,
   That he reacht forth unto me :
No otherwise, then if he would   [*than*
   By dainty things undo me.

He bade me then that Neck-lace use ;
   And told me too, he maketh
A glorious end by such a Noose,
   His Death for Love that taketh.

'Twas but a dream ; but had I been
   There really alone ;
My desp'rate feares, in love, had seen
   Mine Execution.

No difference i' th' dark.[8]

NIGHT makes no difference 'twixt the Priest and
      Clark ;
Jone as my Lady is as good i'th' dark.

The Body.

THE Body is the Soules poore house, or home,
   Whose Ribs the Laths are, & whose Flesh the
      Loame.

[8] See Glossarial Index s. v.

To Sapho.

THOU saist thou lov'st me *Sapho ;* I say no ;
 But would to Love I could beleeve 'twas so !
Pardon my feares (sweet *Sapho*) I desire
That thou be righteous found ; and I the Lyer.

Out of Time, out of Tune.

WE blame, nay, we despise her paines
 That wets her Garden when it raines :
But when the drought has dri'd the knot,[9]
Then let her use the watring-pot.
We pray for showers (at our need)
To drench, but not to drown our seed.

To his Booke.

TAKE mine advise, and go not neere
 Those faces (sower as Vineger.)[1]
For these, and Nobler numbers can
Ne'r please the *supercillious* man.

To his Honour'd Friend, Sir Thomas Heale.[2]

STAND by the *Magick* of my powerfull Rhymes
 'Gainst all the indignation of the Times.

---

[9] = parterre or garden plot.
[1] Shakespeare's " vinegar aspect " (Merchant of Venice, i. 1).
[2] Sir Thomas' Hele, of Fleet, co. Devon, High Sheriff of the

Age shall not wrong thee ; or one jot abate
Of thy both Great, and everlasting fate.
While others perish, here's thy life decreed
Because begot of my *Immortall* seed.

The Sacrifice, by way of Discourse betwixt himselfe and Julia.

Herr. COME and let's in solemn wise
    Both addresse to sacrifice :
Old Religion first commands
That we wash our hearts, and hands.
Is the beast exempt from staine,
Altar cleane, no fire prophane ?
Are the Garlands ? Is the Nard
Ready here ?

Jul.   All well prepar'd,
With the Wine that must be shed
(Twixt the hornes) upon the head,
Of the holy Beast we bring
For our Trespasse-offering.

Herr. All is well ; now next to these
    Put we on pure Surplices ;

county in 1618, died in Nov., 1624. This was probably his son, who was also Sir Thomas. He was created a baronet 28th May, 1627. He was one of the Royalist commanders at the siege of Plymouth : died in November, 1670.

And with Chaplets crown'd, we'l rost
With perfumes the Holocaust :
And (while we the gods invoke)
Reade acceptance by the smoake.

To Apollo.

THOU mighty Lord and master of the Lyre,
   Unshorn [3] *Apollo*, come, and re-inspire
My fingers so, the Lyrick-strings to move,
That I may play, and sing a Hymne to Love.

On Love.

LOVE is a kind of warre :[4] Hence those who feare ;
   No cowards must his royall Ensignes beare.

Another.

WHERE love begins, there dead thy first desire :
   A sparke neglected makes a mighty fire.

An Hymne to Cupid.

THOU, thou that bear'st the sway
   With whom the Sea-Nimphs play ;
And *Venus*, every way :

---

[3] = imberbis or beardless.   See Glossarial Index s. v.

[4] " Militat omnis amans : et habet sua castra Cupido."   Ovid,
Art. Am.   " Vixi puellis nuper idoneus,
         Et militavi non sine gloria." Horace, Od. iii. 26.

When I embrace thy knee ;
And make short pray'rs to thee :
In love, then prosper me.
This day I goe to wooe ;
Instruct me how to doe
This worke thou put'st me too.
From shame my face keepe free,
From scorne I begge of thee,
Love to deliver me :
So shall I sing thy praise ;
And to thee Altars raise,
Unto the end of daies.

To Electra.

LET not thy Tomb-stone er'e be laid by me :
    Nor let my Herse, be wept upon by thee :
But let that instant when thou dy'st be known,
The minute of mine *expiration*.
One knell be rung for both ; and let one grave
To hold us two, an endlesse honour have.

How his soule came ensnared.

MY soule would one day goe and seeke
    For Roses, and in *Julia's* cheeke
A richess of those sweets she found,
(As in another *Rosamond*.)

But gathering Roses as she was ;[5]
(Not knowing what would come to passe)
It chanst a ringlet of her haire,
Caught my poore soule, as in a snare :
Which ever since has been in thrall ;
Yet freedome, shee enjoyes withall.

Factions.

THE factions of the great ones call,
    To side with them, the Commons all.

Kisses Loathsome.

I ABHOR the slimie kisse,
    (Which to me most loathsome is.)
Those lips please me which are plac't
Close, but not too strictly lac't :
Yeilding I wo'd have them; yet
Not a wimbling [6] Tongue admit :
What sho'd poking-sticks[7] make there,
When the ruffe is set elsewhere ?

---

[5] Cf. Tennyson's " Miller's Daughter."
[6] A ' wimble ' is an auger or gimlet.
[7] = sticks for putting the parts of a ruff in a proper form.

Upon Reape.

R*EAPE'S* eyes so rawe are, that (it seemes) the flyes
Mistake the flesh, and flye-blow both his eyes;
So that an Angler, for a daies expence,
May baite his hooke, with maggots taken thence.

Upon Teage.

T*EAGE* has told lyes so long, that when *Teage* tells
Truth, yet *Teages* truths are untruths,[8] (nothing else.)

Upon Julia's *Haire, bundled up in a golden net.*

T ELL me, what needs those rich deceits,
These golden Toyles, and Trammel-nets,[9]
To take thine haires when they are knowne
Already tame, and all thine owne?
'Tis I am wild, and more then haires   [*than*
Deserve these Mashes[1] and those snares.

---

[8] = that which he troweth, but he was like Antonio, one
" Who having unto truth by telling of it
Made such a sinner of his memory
To credit his own lie." Tempest, i. 2.
[9] See Glossarial Index s. e.   [1] = meshes.

Set free thy Tresses, let them flow
As aires doe breathe, or winds doe blow :
And let such curious Net-works be
Lesse set for them, then spred for me.   [*than*

Upon Truggin.

T*RUGGIN* a Footman was; but now, growne
    lame,
Truggin now lives but to belye his name.

END OF VOL. II.

PRINTED BY ROBERT ROBERTS, BOSTON, LINCOLNSHIRE.

BINDING LIST JUL 15 1934

PR
3510
A5G76
1876
v.2

Herrick, Robert
    Complete poems

PLEASE DO NOT REMOVE
CARDS OR SLIPS FROM THIS POCKET

UNIVERSITY OF TORONTO LIBRARY

ImTheStory.com

Personalized Classic Books in many genre's

Unique gift for kids, partners, friends, colleagues

Customize:

- Character Names
- Upload your own front/back cover images (optional)
- Inscribe a personal message/dedication on the
  inside page (optional)

Customize many titles Including
- Alice in Wonderland
- Romeo and Juliet
- The Wizard of Oz
- A Christmas Carol
- Dracula
- Dr. Jekyll & Mr. Hyde
- And more...

Lightning Source UK Ltd.
Milton Keynes UK
UKHW02f0758060918
328419UK00011B/851/P

9 781313 956451